# Breaking the Proactive Paradox

# Breaking the Proactive Paradox

*Maximizing Performance Through Empowerment*

Tim Baker

BUSINESS EXPERT PRESS

*Leader in applied, concise business books*

*Breaking the Proactive Paradox:*
*Maximizing Performance Through Empowerment*

Copyright © Business Expert Press, LLC, 2022.

Cover design by Charlene Kronstedt

Interior design by Exeter Premedia Services Private Ltd., Chennai, India

First published in 2021 by
Business Expert Press, LLC
222 East 46th Street, New York, NY 10017
www.businessexpertpress.com

ISBN-13: 978-1-63742-139-0 (paperback)
ISBN-13: 978-1-63742-140-6 (e-book)

Business Expert Press Human Resource Management
and Organizational Behavior Collection

Collection ISSN: 1946-5637 (print)
Collection ISSN: 1946-5645 (electronic)

First edition: 2021

10 9 8 7 6 5 4 3 2 1

*To the thousands of leaders, I've had the privilege of worked with, who strive to get the best from the people they work with*

# Description

**How do you get your team members to exercise appropriate independent judgment?**

**How do you get employees to be more accountable for their actions?**

Leaders need team members to be empowered and proactive post COVID-19.

What are the roadblocks? How are they overcome? Most books on employee empowerment bypass two critical relationships: the employment compact and the jobholder and their job.

These two relationships hold the key to unlocking employee empowerment.

This breakthrough book is for leaders who want to maximize performance through empowerment. It offers a new approach and practical strategies to energize employees to exercise their initiative when needed and be accountable for their actions.

A proactive employee is engaged in their job and can confidently make decisions without overly relying on their manager.

## Keywords

empowerment; proactive behavior; initiative; independent judgment; employment relationship; psychological contract; performance management; performance

# Contents

# Testimonials

*"Tim has produced another "winner," and this book is chock-full of informative and hands-on advice, which gets at the heart of organizations and their people thriving in a VUCA world. I appreciated his insight that the way work is structured is an overlooked stumbling block to unleashing employee engagement. The need for greater interpersonal communications between managers and their constituents is right-on target, especially in clarifying expectations on the part of both parties and the importance of continuous feedback and dialogue. The book is well-organized, easy to read, and full of practical applications."*—**Barry Z. Posner, PhD, Michael J. Accolti, S.J. Chair and Professor of Leadership, Coauthor, *The Leadership Challenge and Everyday People, Extraordinary Leadership***

*"Effective leaders use their power to empower others; their strengths to strengthen others. The ideas and tools in this excellent book help make this happen by proactively navigating the paradoxes that shape work today."* —**Dave Ulrich, Rensis Likert Professor, Ross School of Business, University of Michigan, Partner, The RBL Group**

# Acknowledgments

Thanks to David Kelly for editing the final chapter and providing the leadership profile tool. I also acknowledge Scott Isenberg, managing executive editor of *Business Expert Press*, for showing faith in the ideas in this book and guiding me through the editorial process so professionally. Thank-you to Dave Ulrich and Barry Posner for their endorsements for the book.

# Introduction

If all your team members were empowered, using sensible independent judgment, and displaying appropriate initiative, what difference would that make? What difference would it make to team performance? What difference would it make to morale, engagement, and job satisfaction? What if you could make empowerment work?

There's a plethora of popular management books and leadership development programs brimming with tactics and methods to inspire employees to be more proactive. These practices are mostly ineffective, however. Why?

Conventional empowerment methods sidestep two workplace relationships. It's these two relationships that hold the key to solving the employee empowerment puzzle. The interaction between the leader and the team members is one of these crucial relationships. The other is the relationship between the jobholder and the work they are tasked to do. Popular management advice assumes that the employment relationship and the way jobs are designed aren't factors in generating greater empowerment. So, the stock standard recommendations we read and hear about are tactics and methods to coax the employee to take more control and responsibility for their work. These well-meaning "solutions" usually fail because they miss the point. The way the manager and employee interact and the way the employee interacts with their work are dodged. But they hold the key to success.

Why is *Breaking the Proactive Paradox* different from other books on the topic? What am I offering you that the others aren't?

Read on.

The post-Covid-19 environment and the renewed interest in working remotely are a timely opportunity for a rethink about employee empowerment. *How can managers and employees collaborate to promote—not inhibit—enterprise? How can jobs be redesigned to foster employee initiative?* These two questions demand our attention now. I deal with them both in *Breaking the Proactive Paradox.*

Most leaders want team members to act proactively in certain circum-stances. Leaders get irritated when a team member sits on their hands and doesn't show appropriate initiative. But the truth is most people are willing (and able) to exercise independent judgment at work. After all, people are proactive at home. Why not at work?

Employees get irritated with managers too. They get frustrated when they don't get the opportunity to act autonomously and independently. This is commonly referred to as micromanagement. So, the manager is annoyed with the employee who won't act proactively. And the employee is annoyed with the manager who won't permit them to act proactively. This is what I call the "proactive paradox."

The main barrier to breaking the proactive paradox is the conventional working relationship between manager and employee, often referred to as the "psychological contract." The traditional psychological contract is characterized by a clear demarcation of responsibility; managers think, and employees do. Yes, but that's all changed now, I hear you say. You think so? I think not.

Although the long-established employment relationship is changing slowly, the beliefs and expectations employees and managers have of each other are deeply entrenched. These ingrained beliefs put the brakes on change. What's more, powerful vested interest—such as trade unions and employer groups—perpetuates the *them and us* employment relationship.

But in a climate of accelerated change and uncertainty, performing is increasingly tied to fostering the enterprising qualities of people at work.

Empowered employees are better for workplaces. But it's not just business that prosper from empowered employees. People who can exercise some reasonable autonomy at work have higher job satisfaction, are more engaged, perform better, and have greater commitment.

Dr. Allan Lee and colleagues conducted a meta-study that found that while empowerment didn't have much effect on routine tasks, it does improve creativity (Lee, Willis, and Wei Tan 2017).[1] When taking more control and responsibility for their work, the employee feels safer expressing their creativity at work. What's more, the research shows that empowered employees were more willing to help their colleagues, volunteer for extra assignments, and likely to support the business beyond their job responsibilities.

Aaron De Smet, a senior partner at McKinsey, challenges the myth that empowering employees means leaving them alone (De Smet, Hewes, and Weiss 2020).[2] The "helicopter boss," who swoops in to fix problems when things go wrong, isn't empowering. Neither is micromanaging. De Smet suggests that to truly empower others, leaders should give employees the space to experience some autonomy, but also hold them accountable if problems arise. I agree. He recommends leaders avoid fixing issues and instead ask questions or offer options when employees come looking for help.

> Genuine empowerment requires leaders to be involved, to be of service, to coach and mentor, to guide, to inspire—it means frequent, highly involved interactions, just of a different nature than the autocratic and controlling style.

This is a good start. But there's more to it than that. People need frameworks, just as trains need train tracks.

*Breaking the Proactive Paradox* paves the way for a new approach to maximizing employee performance. More than ever, applying independent judgment to solve complex problems and dilemmas is inexorably linked to work performance.

Part I defines the proactive paradox and its origins. The proactive framework is discussed in Part II. These four strategies: shared purpose, boundary management, information exchange, and proactive accountability are applied to clarify (you'll hear that word a lot!) where proactive thinking is expected … and not expected. This framework supports the psychologically safe work setting for people to act autonomously and use their independent judgment. Part III tackles the way we design work. Job specification (the century-old job design mechanism we still use today) is a euphemism for dumbing down work and limiting enterprise. To augment job specification and lessen its negative impact on empowerment, job crafting is a promising way for jobholders to reshape their work to better suit their needs and strengths. And Part IV offers leaders a methodology for assessing their application of the proactive framework in the workplace.

I'm sure you have the best intentions. You may have read all the books; gone to the seminars and workshops. But unless you deal with these two workplace relationships: the one between you and your team members and the one between the team members and their work, it will be one step forward and two steps backward. That, I can promise you. But I think part of you knows this.

I can also promise you a new way forward—the missing piece in the jigsaw puzzle.

# PART I

# The Proactive Paradox

# CHAPTER 1

# What Is the Proactive Paradox?

Giving and accepting autonomy is now paramount, despite the impediments the traditional employment relationship imposes.

*Sam is a team leader in a web development business. He has been promoted recently based on his superior technical know-how. Sam reminds his five team members at their weekly WIP meeting that he expects them to show initiative when dealing with their clients' web development challenges. This message is well received.*

*Despite his good intentions, Sam has trouble letting go of the work—he enjoys the technical challenges and is a good web designer. Brad, one of Sam's team members, also enjoys being a technical expert and the autonomy that role promises. But he notices Sam likes to meddle in technical decisions and sometimes overrides the work his team does.*

*Brad assumes therefore that Sam wants to be consulted on most decisions, despite being very capable to make his own decisions. Brad checks-in with Sam regularly and relies on Sam to make the final call. Sam is becoming frustrated by how dependent Brad is on him for answers, even though he's oblivious of how much me jumps in to make technical decisions.*

*Being frustrated with the lack of initiative Brad is showing in his job, Sam decides to override Brad on several important decisions on clients' work. He assumes that he needs to do this, since Brad seems too reactive and incapable or unwilling to think for himself, always checking with him how things should be done. From Brad's point-of-view, this interference reinforces his view that this is the way Sam prefers it, even though he is irritated. Sam is also exasperated because he thinks Brad could show more independent judgment.*

Being proactive means "taking an active and self-starting approach to work and going beyond what is formally required in a given job" (Mind-Tools).[1] I use terms such as *initiative, enterprise, autonomy,* and *independent judgment* interchangeably throughout this book to describe proactive behavior. And proactive behavior is a large part of feeling empowered. Donald Campbell, professor of management, in his article "The Proactive Employee: Managing Workplace Initiative" (Campbell 2000),[2] coined the term the "initiative paradox." I have developed his initial idea in *Breaking the Proactive Paradox.*

Why isn't proactive employee behavior common practice in the world of work? There's a glut of books, countless seminars, and proliferating podcasts on tools and techniques for managers to make empowerment work, as I said in the introduction. But most of this well-meaning information is misguided. This advice bypasses the barriers blocking empowerment. Instead of enabling helpful proactive behavior, the employee is in most cases conditioned to react to their boss's impulses. Why? What's stopping people from using more independent judgment? These well-intended recommendations in the management advice industry don't address the engrained obstacles inhibiting proactive behavior at work.

Campbell defined the initiative paradox as follows:

> Wanting employees to use judgment and initiative, while also wanting their judgment to mirror the manager's own, thus producing anticipated, predictable results (Campbell 2000).[3]

I have a slightly different take on this. To me, the proactive paradox occurs this way: Managers and employees are on the same page to start with. The manager expects the employee to use their independent judgment in the right circumstances. The employee too wants to exercise autonomy in certain situations; they don't want to be told what to do all the time. There is a breakdown in communication. The manager and employee end up frustrated with one another, despite wanting the same thing.

Observing their manager, the employee gets the signal that their boss likes being in-charge; they want to run the show their way. Although the manager talks about *collaboration* and *empowerment,* the employee observes the opposite behavior from their boss. What the manager says and what they do are inconsistent. Seeing the manager's authoritative behavior, the employee sits on their hands and waits to be *told* what to do, or at least doesn't initiate action.

The manager observes the employee's passive conduct, even though they claim they are prepared to use independent judgment to make decisions. So, the manager feels frustrated too with the inconsistence they see between what's said and done. In response to this, the manager fills the vacuum of inaction from the employee. They start making more decisions and become more directive in areas where the employee is not showing initiative, in other words. However, it's in these areas that the employee is willing (given the opportunity) to be proactive. But they feel discouraged to do so, nonetheless. Observing what they consider interference, the employee's impression of the manager's authoritarian tendency is confirmed.

Despite the manager's rhetoric of shared leadership and participation, the employee now realizes the manager wasn't genuine in these assertions. The manager's actions suggest otherwise; they don't really want the employee to show initiative after all. This paradox is like a dog chasing after its tail. Although entertaining for a while, it ends in disappointment.

What then are the origins of this proactive paradox?

The traditional employment relationship, also referred to as the psychological contract, was born out of the Industrial Revolution, over 200 years ago. Scientific management arrived on the scene approximately 100 years ago, popularized on the Ford Motor Company assembly line. Frederick Taylor, one of the architects of scientific management, got productivity boosts by applying this concept in Henry Ford's business. Scientific management became the flavor of the month and is still operating today in most organizations across all industries, including McDonalds and other successful franchise operations. The conventional psychological contract combined with its bed fellow, scientific management, further entrenched a "them and us" relationship between employer and employee.

The *them and us* relationship—briefly translated as the manager doing the *thinking* and the worker doing the *work*—is familiar to all of us, even though it's 100 plus years since the birth of scientific management. Even with an avalanche of "modern" management books and the leadership seminars and workshops, this relationship is deeply rooted in industry. It's therefore challenging to change, even though it's no longer relevant. This old employment relationship persists—despite all the commentary that it "last century." At its heart, the traditional employment relationship is based on the idea that the manager's role is to plan, and the worker's role is to follow that plan.

This established manager–employee relationship has a tidy separation of duties and responsibilities. This arrangement—what has arguably worked well in the past—impedes the enterprising qualities of employees. And it is these qualities that are now prized in a less stable and unpredictable marketplace.

Until the fundamental roles in the employment relationship are transformed, empowering employees—even with their desire to exercise more freedom and autonomy in most cases—is counterproductive. The proactive paradox is like a military officer barking an order to their subordinates to show more independent judgment. It falls on deaf ears.

But a word of caution: Changing the dynamics of the oldest relationship in industry is more difficult that it appears. This old psychological contract is enduring and pervasive. A shift from an adversarial relationship to a collaborative partnership—overdue undoubtedly—is a big leap to make. Old habits die hard.

Does that mean we shouldn't try? Absolutely not! But we must start by acknowledging reality and not assuming we'll all moved on and already evolved into a different type of working relationship.

This transformation starts with you, the leader. Leaders need to rethink their role and the way they interact with those they lead. Until this occurs, nothing essentially changes. Enterprising behavior displays of prudent initiative and encouraging employees to be proactive will be asphyxiated without fresh thinking. Superficial techniques aren't sustainable against a backdrop of the them and us working relationship. All these well-intended tools and practices drummed into us at seminars and workshops won't cut through until a new kind of employment relationship is formed.

*Breaking the Proactive Paradox* does offer you some strategies to stimulate employee empowerment, like the other books you've read. But there's a difference. I first want you to understand the deeply entrenched

# Where the Rubber Meets the Road

### Covid-19 Lockdown

During the Covid-19 lockdown, where most employees were forced to work from home—many still doing so, perhaps permanently—managers couldn't supervise closely, at least in terms of proximity. Employees were compelled, due to their isolation, to think for themselves. Leaders I spoke with during lockdown were pleasantly surprised by the level of enterprise shown by their team members. Many employees I spoke to relish this opportunity to exercise more initiative, with the boss not breathing down their neck. They could decide when they worked, what they worked on, and how they got their tasks done. A recent survey of 5,000 workers shows that two-thirds say they are more productive working from home than in an office (Citrix 2020).[4] Perhaps, the pandemic is altering the employment relationship? It remains to be seen whether this is just an aberration in the post-Covid environment.

roadblocks that choke employee enterprise. Without this understanding, nothing will change, at least not in a sustainable way. The proactive paradox is a symptom of the way managers and employees have traditionally interacted. Let's diagnose the problem before offering the treatment.

Another difference in my book is that the strategies I offer you are a way to transform your working relationship with your team members—it's not only about getting more displays of initiative. By tackling the main barrier—the conventional employment relationship—it promises to unleash the enterprising qualities employees generally want to exercise at work.

In other words, the book does more than offer you some tactics to change your behavior so that your team members will change their behavior. The way the manager and employee typically relate to one another is the problem—and the solution. A symptom of this perpetual them and us relationship is the proactive paradox. The answer to generating more employee empowerment is breaking the proactive paradox. And to do this, the emphasis needs to be on how the manager and employee communicate with one another.

We'll explore this relationship and its drawbacks in a little more depth in the next chapter.

After understanding the employment relationship—in both what it has traditionally been and what it can to be—you'll be better placed to appreciate why the proactive paradox is commonplace. The proactive paradox model (Chapter 4) illustrates where the communication breakdown occurs, and why. All this helps explain why getting employees to be proactive is a bigger struggle than it should be.

The irony, as I've mentioned, is that the manager and the employee generally want proactive behavior to flourish in their workplace. Many managers—not all—want employees to exercise their initiative, think for themselves, use their independent judgment, and be enterprising. And most employees—again, not all—want to have some autonomy to make decisions and not be too reliant on the boss. But the traditional psychological contract gets in the way of this mutual aim.

Managers ask me all the time: *How do I get my team members to show more (or any) initiative?* But employees I talk to often ask me: *Why won't my manager allow me to be more autonomous and trust me to take more initiative?* That's the paradox!

So, the central questions I address in *Breaking the Proactive Paradox* are as follows:

- What is blocking this shared aim?
- And what can be done about it?

When the two partners want the same thing and when they both don't get what they want, it creates mistrust and further erodes employee empowerment. Frustration inevitably results. This irritation occurs when both partners don't get what they want. Managers want employees to take an active and self-starter approach to their work and going beyond what is formally required in their job. Being too reliant on their boss exasperates a progressive leader. But the enlightened employee gets upset too when they have no autonomy. They want more freedom to think for themselves and feel stifled by a controlling boss. This situation is like a Mexican standoff, both parties are waiting for the other to make the first move.

Both entities in the employment relationship want the same thing because it benefits them. Empowered employees have higher job satisfaction, are more engaged, perform better, and have greater commitment. And managers generally don't want to be making decisions that should be made by their team members. A proactive employee lessens the load on their manager. The employee who is prepared to use sensible independent judgment spreads the onus of decision-making responsibility. Sharing the leadership role is appealing to a collaborative leader. This is even more attractive when the proactive employee is prepared to be accountable for their actions. It frees up the manager's time. Taking ownership of the tasks that need doing decreases the manager's burden; they don't feel the pressure to make all the decisions. I should state that not all managers—even when it is exercised wisely—view proactive employee behavior as helpful. But most do.

What's more, the type and degree of proactive behavior that's tolerable vary from manager to manager. Some managers, for instance, may want to be informed in advance of a decision one of their team members is prepared to make. This gives the manager the opportunity to either curtail or prevent the proposed action. On the other hand, another manager may be delighted that a team member took the initiative and after taking it, happy to be updated. Apart from the manager's acceptance of employee initiative, it can also depend on the type of decision too.

Apart from the manager's preference and their tolerance to proactive behavior, the channels of communication will largely be dependent on the type of initiative and the risks associated with it. Even with these variations, I have yet to meet a manager who—in theory at least—thinks that an employee willing to think for themselves is a bad idea.

What about the employee?

Employees are generally prepared to act proactively and use independent judgment. People do this away from the workplace. So why would it be different in the workplace? Like managers, the extent and limits of empowerment vary from person to person, depending on the individual, their capabilities, and the situation they face at the time. Professionals and skilled workers, for instance, are trained to use their judgment in day-to-day problem-solving. Their training provides them with the necessary know-how to solve problems without constantly checking upline. Nonetheless, the extent to which they exercise independent judgment—apart from their relationship with their manager—is dependent on their confidence, experience, and capability.

At any rate, expertise gives the knowledge worker license to deal with challenges independently in their field of expertise. As Daniel Pink says in in his book *Drive: The Surprising Truth About What Motivates Us* (Pink 2011),[5] knowledge workers need three things from their leader to be inspired: *autonomy, mastery,* and *purpose*. These three requirements foster intrinsic motivation, according to Pink. The main reason a person studies for a qualification is so they can use their judgment in the work they're qualified to do.

Autonomy refers to giving employees the opportunity to organize and make their own decisions about the work they do. The degree of autonomy an employee will accept will vary, as mentioned before. But the knowledge worker is undoubtedly motivated to some degree by having some autonomy over their work. Mastery is about building the employee's skills and capacity to do the work capably. The leader's role is therefore to provide their team members with the necessary learning and development they need to continue to grow and develop. And purpose is communicating to the employee the reason for the task and how it contributes to the strategic direction of the organization. This is what Simon Sinek refers to as the *why* of work. More about these three attributes are discussed later.

As I said earlier, it should be acknowledged that a minority of employees don't want to think for themselves, just as some managers don't want employees to act independently. But this is the exception rather than the rule in both cases. I should add that this fixed mindset is career limiting. Managers who have a reputation as a control freak will increasingly find it harder to advance to senior leadership roles. And employees who want to be spoon-fed by their manager face extinction in the 21st-century workplace. Giving and accepting autonomy is paramount now, despite the impediments the traditional employment relationship imposes.

In the next chapter, we explore this them and us relationship in detail to understand the psychological barriers at play that create the proactive paradox.

# Top 10 Points

1. Being proactive means taking an active and self-starting approach to work and going beyond what is formally required in a job.
2. The traditional employment relationship, also referred to as the psychological contract, was born out of the Industrial Revolution, over 200 years ago.
3. This established manager–employee relationship has a tidy separation of duties and responsibilities.
4. Until the fundamental roles in the employment relationship are transformed, empowering employees—even with their desire to exercise more freedom and autonomy in most cases—is counterproductive.
5. This transformation starts with the leader.
6. The irony is that the manager and the employee generally want proactive behavior to flourish in the workplace.
7. When the two partners want the same thing and when they both don't get what they want, it creates mistrust and further erodes employee empowerment.
8. Expertise gives the knowledge worker license to deal with challenges independently in their field of expertise.
9. It should be acknowledged that a minority of employees don't want to think for themselves, just as some managers don't want employees to act independently.
10. This fixed mindset is now career limiting.

# CHAPTER 2

# The Them and Us Relationship

…we need to get employees to bring their brain to work with them
and not feel bound to leave it in a paper bag at the gate.

*Travis is a progressive manager. He wants to work with his team col-*
*laboratively. Travis's leadership style is based on dialog with his team*
*when the situation calls for it. He not only wants but also expects team*
*members to use their independent judgment when the situation war-*
*rants it. However, Jerry, one of Travis's team members, has a conser-*
*vative belief about management and employees and their roles. Jerry*
*believes it's the manager's primary responsibility to make decisions;*
*after all, in his mind, that's what the boss gets paid to do. Furthermore,*
*Jerry sees his role as getting on and doing what has been asked of him*
*by the boss, in his case Travis. He, therefore, doesn't think it's his role to*
*exercise independent judgment. Furthermore, he views conversations*
*and open dialog with Travis as mostly unnecessary and even a waste of*
*time. These differing unwritten expectations result in some frustration*
*between Travis and Jerry. However, in their own ways, they both are*
*trying to fulfill what they understand to be their responsibilities.*

In the previous chapter, I stated that the traditional employee–manager relationship is the biggest obstacle to empowering people at work.
Here, I want to explore why I think this is the case. There's a transition
from the old employment contract I characterize as the them and us taking place, but it's slow and painful. The remnants of this them and us
relationship are, however, still evident across most industries.

You've undoubtedly witnessed this traditional working relationship in
your career. To better understand this employment relationship, we've all

been exposed to, I will illustrate eight shared beliefs and expectations that define it. This awareness helps explain why it's the main stumbling block for empowerment to flourish in today's workplace. Furthermore, a closer inspection of this over 200-plus-year-old psychological contract is useful to realize why proactive employee behavior isn't commonplace. The proactive paradox I discussed in the previous chapter is a symptom of this psychological contract. This them and us relationship leads to frustration now that we need people to use their independent judgment more and more. So, the major obstacle is the outdated psychological contract, where employees still refer to management as *them* and themselves as *us*, and vice versa.

## Psychological Contract

What then is meant by the term *psychological contract*, and how is it relevant to empowerment? This psychological contract has existed since the dawn of industry. Even with the mantra of a more collaboration between managers and employees we read about, the characteristics of them and us is still prevalent to some degree in most contemporary businesses.

The traditional employment relationship—like all relationships—hinges on a set of shared beliefs between management and labor. In the next chapter, I introduce you to a model of a new working relationship that is conducive to resolving the proactive paradox. This new employment relationship is diametrically opposite to the old contract. A new contract is pivotal to developmental and performance conversations between the leader and team members. This dialog is the catalyst where ideas are generated, innovation thrives, and knowledge is created and shared.

With a new contract, more issues are dealt with collaboratively, where the drive for improvement is stronger than the fear of failure. This shared leadership model is supported by an entirely different set of common beliefs and expectations.

But before we consider this new model, we need to take a closer look at the old model and its shortcomings in promoting initiative and enterprising behavior.

A psychological contract can be defined as a set of unwritten expectations between employees and managers. Employees have a reasonably fixed set of beliefs about the role of management. And managers have certain generalized expectations of employees. In other words, a psychological contract is based on a set of beliefs both entities have about the role of the other party.

To illustrate, employees expect to be paid on time, be treated with respect, and be given a fair go by their manager. If employees don't believe their managers are upholding these basic expectations, the psychological contract has been breached. Management, in other words, has failed to live up to their side of the unwritten agreement and consequently infringed the contract.

On the other hand, managers have a customary expectation that employees will work hard, cause few problems, and arrive and leave work punctually. From the manager's perspective, if an employee's behavior is inconsistent with this, they have violated the contract. These beliefs (there are many more) have been handed down from generation to generation, with no real substantial change.

Where do most managers learn their management skills? From their managers. And who manages the managers? Those who were previously in those managers' roles. Likewise, employees learn from watching and listening to more experienced employees; they learn what to expect from management. It's little wonder, therefore, that these beliefs have remained static for so long.

Since the 1980s, the traditional psychological contract has been unraveling, however. Younger employees have vastly different expectations of work than previous generations typically had. *Millennials*, for instance, expect to be more involved in the decision-making processes than *baby boomers*. Older employees generally expect to be given clear instructions on the work that needs to be done without the same expectation of being consulted. It's wrong to generalize about generations though. Many baby boomers have shifted their beliefs and expectations over the years in response to cultural change, education, and their own life circumstances. And it's true that some millennials can be quite traditional in their outlook. But these different generational expectations have had some impact.

Management beliefs are changing too, particularly since that later part of the last century. Most managers now anticipate that employees will demonstrate appropriate initiative when a situation warrants it, for instance. Several decades ago, managers held a different view. In the past, they valued compliance over enterprise.

Today's workplace is full of these conflicting beliefs about the role of management and labor. The psychological contract is undergoing a painful transition from the old to the new. The boundaries around expectations are blurred. This ambiguity—a relatively recent phenomenon—has led to communication breakdowns, loss of trust between managers and employees, and the proactive paradox.

This uncertainty has given rise to the proactive paradox. It raises questions for the manager: Should I involve employees in the decision-making process, or do they want me to make unilateral decisions? Where do I draw the line between making decisions and involving my team members in these decisions? Employees have questions too: Does my manager want me to be compliant or enterprising? Does my manager want me to show independent judgment and if so, when, and where? Without clear answers to these questions, frustration and mistrust inevitably occur.

The disproportionate power between manager and employee makes it more confusing. Managers fail to raise these questions for fear of being perceived as indecisive. There's often reluctance from the employee too to raise these issues for a concern that they may appear incompetent. So, clarifying the boundaries around when proactive behavior is appropriate and when it's not, don't get discussed. Interactions are limited to task-specific matters.

A manager embracing the old contract will view developmental, non-project-specific conversations as a waste of their time. Or, at the very least, they won't have a priority over getting the product out the door or the service delivered. And a traditional thinking employee will undoubtedly shirk this type of interaction with their boss. What's more, they probably won't think it's their role to collaborate. Having a relatively equal say with their boss on a host of matters is counter to their expectation of how the relationship should work. Besides, in their view, these conversations are about decisions the manager should make. With a them and us mindset, developmental conversations will be avoided.

Managers adopting a command-and-control style of leadership won't value employee initiative to the same extent as a collaborative leader does. The idea of the employee displaying their independent judgment is threatening to a controlling manager. In reverse, the employee who believe it's the manager's job to direct them won't be willing to act autonomously. If both the manager and employee are in sync, discussions about where and when initiative should take place are irrelevant, or at least a low priority. They share an understanding that the boss's role is to make decisions and the employee's role is to follow their instructions.

With this outdated belief system, proactive employee behavior isn't valued by either party. However, this psychological barrier is exacerbated when there's misalignment between the expectation of both entities. The case at the beginning of this chapter illustrates this discord.

---

## Where the Rubber Meets the Road

### Misalignment in Expectations

Mary expects as part of a team that she will be consulted and involved in decision making from time-to-time on work-related issues. She believes that Jenny, her manager, ought to share the responsibilities for decision making with her team. Jenny, however, has a different belief.

Jenny thinks that the lines of responsibility between herself and her team are crystal clear. In her mind, the manager's role is to make decisions and the team member's job is to follow her instructions and carry out the work. Mary finds it exasperating that Jenny is unwilling to engage the team in discussions. She is keen to discuss her ideas with Jenny. But Jenny is not at all receptive to any of her ideas or suggestions.

Mary is willing to act proactively when the opportunity arises. But Jenny doesn't believe in collaborative leadership. She views her role differently. Jenny thinks being decisive and communicating these decisions clearly to employees in good leadership. Jenny thinks this is being accountable and professional. In private, Mary labels Jenny as a micromanager. Proper proactive behavior is suppressed due to this discord between Mary and Jenny. Two well-intentioned people find themselves mutually locked out of a more productive working relationship because of a conflicted psychological contract.

Workplaces are full of these silent conflicts—disagreements based on differing views of the role of manager and employee. It's these contradictions that contribute to the proactive paradox. And because this is a *psychological* contract—one that existing in the mind and not on paper—these disagreements and misunderstandings rarely, if ever, get discussed.

Before defining a model conducive to collaboration and enterprise, let's look more closely at the underpinning beliefs of this traditional psychological contract. I will illustrate how these shared beliefs negatively impact employee empowerment. This model will give you some indicators to better understand the problem. Moreover, the model serves three useful purposes. First, it illustrates the inadequacy of the them and us relationship to function in a fast-moving, dynamic marketplace requiring independent judgment. Second, the model helps to sharpen the distinction between the old and new psychological contracts. And third, it provides a set of useful benchmarks to measure progress toward the new employment relationship. Navigating where we need to go is best done by understanding where we've come from.

Table 2.1 summarizes eight shared beliefs, the supporting expectations of the manager and employee, and the implications for proactive behavior.

The left-hand column identifies eight shared beliefs, based on my research. These beliefs are the essential elements of the traditional psychological contract. They are embraced by both the employee and their manager.

In the employee column, the brief descriptors summarize the expectations a traditional employee has of their manager. If the manager honors these expectations through their word and deed, the employee will be satisfied. But if a manager violates any of these expectations, the employee will consider the contract breached.

The manager column illustrates their conventional expectations of the employee. If the employee's behavior is consistent with their expectations, they are satisfied. But if the expectations are broken by an employee, the manager will consider the contract broken.

When the employee and manager's expectations of the other are fulfilled, the traditional psychological contract is preserved and strengthened. The mutual fulfillment of these expectations reinforces the beliefs

*Table 2.1 Traditional employment relationship model (Baker 2014)[1]*

| Shared belief | Employee's expectation of the manager | Manager's expectation of the employee | Implication for proactive behavior |
|---|---|---|---|
| Specialized employment | To provide me with clearly defined job boundaries | To complete your job requirements | A narrow and clearly defined role minimizes the need for proactive behavior |
| Internal focus | To provide me with clear policies and procedures to follow | To follow clearly defined policies and procedures | Clear policies and procedures leave little scope for independent judgment |
| Job focus | To describe to me the requirements of the job in a document | To fulfill the obligations of the job description | Following the literal requirements of the job description leaves little room for autonomy |
| Functional-based work | To place me with others in the same functional role | To work co-operatively within a functional area | Functional work, with its standard operating procedures, minimizes the need for independent judgment |
| Human dispirit and work | To offer me stable and secure employment above all, even if the work is repetitive and mundane | To follow directions, complete the work, and don't complain | Going through the motions of completing a narrow and repetitive set of tasks reduces engagement and enterprise |
| Loyalty | To show me loyalty for my length of service and faithfully following systems, processes, and practices | To demonstrate loyalty by adhering to the employer's systems, processes, and practices | Loyalty means faithfully following the organization's way of doing things over thinking for oneself |
| Training | To provide me with adequate training to do my job | To learn your job effectively | Development centers around technical training to master the job and its specific obligations only |
| Closed information | To give me the necessary information to do my job | To apply the information needed to do your job | Limiting information to job requirements restricts independent decision making |

in the left-hand column. Alternatively, if any of these responses aren't fulfilled by either entity, the psychological contract is broken temporarily or permanently.

The column on the far right summarizes the implications for proactive behavior when the beliefs are met by both parties. It illustrates that this psychological contract, at best, discourages initiative and independent judgment from the employee.

## A Process of Mutual Exchange

At the heart of any one-to-one relationship—be it personal or professional—is a mutual exchange between two people. Basically, this exchange in the customary employment relationship consists of a manager communicating work requirements and—in return for a willingness to comply—the worker receives a wage. This has been the conventional lynchpin of the employment relationship since the birth of industry. Any failure to meet a work instruction, or payment of the agreed wage, is a contract infringement. In this kind of relationship, with clear roles and responsibilities, employee empowerment is limited.

Despite this shortcoming, the traditional employment relationship is easy to follow. What's more, it has arguably worked well and survived since the 19th century.[2] This psychological contract, the one I illustrated in Table 2.1, is, in some measure, still observable in many workplaces today. And with the power of social conditioning, it's inherently part of people's working life. In short, the employment relationship is the most significant relationship in people's working career. Partners change from time to time as managers and employees come and go, but fundamentally, the psychological contract remains.

Its longevity and our personal experience in the employment lifecycle (most often lasting over 40 years) have entrenched the contract. It's, therefore, more challenging to transform, despite what some management consultants may think. Nonetheless, it needs to change. To meet the challenges and opportunities the global economy, we have little choice. These external pressures—pressures only evident in a past few decades—have been the catalyst for an ad hoc transition from the old to the new. Unsurprisingly, this shift has caused a state of confusion.

While the traditional contract is straightforward, people are complicated, and the work pressures they now face are increasingly complex. Simplistic solutions won't work in a sustainable way. I think people, in particular, younger workers, are aware of the need for a new dynamic—one that's more collaborative than confrontational. But there are also powerful forces inhibiting change. Pressure groups like trade unions and employer associations, for example, are done their best to extent the them and us relationship to protect their own interests.

Nonetheless, the basic idea that it's the manager's job to make decisions and the employee's job to complete a set of tasks is obsolete and therefore an inadequate way to address the challenges of volatility, uncertainty, complexity, and ambiguity (VUCA).[3] Over a 100 years ago, Henry Ford said, "Why is it every time I ask for a pair of hands they come attached to a brain?" (Jacobs 2020).[4] This separation of responsibilities (managers *think* and employees *do*) creates a dilemma. People who are never given responsibility never become responsible. And if employees are given limited responsibility to think, the greater the burden of accountability on the manager's shoulders. Instead of tinkering at the edges with superficial and unsustainable tactics, we need to find a way of fundamentally altering the way managers and employees relate to one another. Furthermore, we need employees to bring their brain to work with them and not feel bound to leave it in a paper bag at the gate.

With an unpredictable and ever-changing marketplace, and the necessity this brings to be adaptable, the answer to resolving this dilemma may seem obvious. Surely, a less formal employment relationship—where the manager allows the employee the freedom to be flexible and innovative in doing their job—is the way forward. This approach is widely advocated in the popular management books. But it's not that simple.

A more informal arrangement, with overlapping responsibilities, will undoubtedly bring with it unwelcomed forms of independent judgment. It also invites forms of manipulation. On one side of the coin, an employee displaying appropriate initiative may be quick to take credit for this. That's fine. No problem. But on the flip side, that same employee could just as easily cite a lack of clear management direction for failing to show enterprising behavior when required. These gray areas are lessened in the traditional contract. But this conventional arrangement can be exploited too. The employee may argue that if it's not on my job description, then I don't need to do it—and not doing something is easily defended by the "work to rules" employee.

Another potential problem with a more fluid working relationship is that managers may feel threatened. They may feel insecure leading others in a more ambiguous arrangement. What's more, they may feel confronted by a proactive team member who they regard as not know their "place." Although perhaps enthusiastic initially, a conservative manager, before too long, will return to the simpler separation of responsibilities in the old arrangement. And this reversion will certainly quash any subsequent attempts by their team to think independently.

So, the challenge is to frame a new working relationship with the same clarity as the traditional employment relationship, but without the same rigid separation of responsibilities. That sounds paradoxical too, right? Bear with me. In this new contract, unlike the traditional one, managers don't delegate and supervise tasks to the same extent. Employees are expected to take greater responsibility and be more accountable for the team output. But unless the new expectations are clear and both parties willing to hold each other to account, a new way of working together will lead to confusion.

Executed well, the good news is that this new working arrangement benefits everyone. In our rapidly changing world of work, the bad news is that there's increasingly little choice other than to say in saying goodbye to the old mindset. The new model I explain in the next chapter is the foundation for resolving the proactive paradox.

Employees mostly want to use their independent judgment in the work they do; they also want meaningful work and to be engaged in that work. Given the opportunity to exercise their enterprising qualities, employees will prosper and so will the business. A work setting will undoubtedly be a happy and productive place if its people are encouraged to work collaboratively on tasks they find fulfilling. Employees working collaboratively with their manager and exercising their initiative when necessary are going to be more responsiveness to fluctuations in market conditions. This gives the business a competitive edge.

To conclude, without a sustainable move away from this traditional psychological contract, the proactive paradox will prevail. The old psychological contract I refer to as the them and us relationship is the major impediment to promoting proactive employee behavior. The established demarcation of roles and responsibilities and the power structure supporting this unwritten contract suppress enterprise and limit productivity. We need to finally discard what has worked well for two centuries and reform the working relationship with less rigidity and more cooperation. This will unleash the full potential of people at work.

In the next chapter, we look more closely at this new contract.

# Top 10 Points

1. The traditional employment relationship—like all relationships—hinges on a set of shared beliefs between management and labor.
2. The psychological contract can be defined as a set of unwritten expectations between employees and managers.
3. Since the 1980s, the traditional psychological contract has been unraveling.
4. A manager embracing the old contract will view developmental, nonproject-specific conversations as a waste of their time.
5. Managers believing in the command-and-control style of leadership won't value employee initiative to the extent as a collaborative leader does.
6. Despite this shortcoming, the traditional employment relationship is easy to follow.
7. While the traditional contract is straightforward, people are complicated, and the work pressures they face are increasingly complex.
8. The challenge is to frame a new working relationship with the same clarity as the traditional employment relationship, but without the same rigid separation of responsibilities.
9. Employees mostly want to use their independent judgment in the work they do; they also want meaningful work and to be engaged in that work.
10. Without a sustainable move away from this traditional psychological contract, the proactive paradox will prevail.

# CHAPTER 3

# The Collaborative Relationship

The old and new models serve as reference points to make
sense of this shifting employment relationship dynamic.

*The newly appointed CEO in the government agency, Samantha,
identifies as her first major challenge as breaking down the boundaries between departments. She observes that the agency is
organized around several "silos"—it's a typically bureaucracy. This is
evident even at the senior management level. The most important cross-
functional team—the senior management team—is disjointed and
not operating as a team. Managers arrive at executive meetings with
their functional "hat" on and fail to consider issues from the perspective of the overall organization. Samantha knows she has a problem
and has her work cut out.*

*She notices the level of cooperation between departments is negligible,
even nonexistent, in some cases. Samantha is determined to change
this. Instead of cooperation there is rivalry.*

*She decides to form several cross-functional project teams. One team
is formed to look at improving communication across the agency, for
example. Representatives are chosen by the new CEO from all six
departments. Another cross-functional project team is set up to review
and improve several archaic systems and processes that are not consistent across the agency.*

*Peter, from the marketing department, is invited by Samantha to
be part of one of these project teams. He is enthusiastic about being
asked to participate, recognizing the need to improve cross-functional
communication throughout the organization. Peter goes to talk to the*

*marketing manager in her office. Mary is apathetic when Peter tells her about this development.*

*"I wish the CEO had spoken to me first," Mary said to Peter in response to the news. "I can't afford to release you to attend these 'talk fests.' Peter, you are too valuable to the department. We're already short-staffed. How often does she want you to attend these meetings?"*

*"I don't know," replied Peter. "She hasn't told me yet."*

*"Well, it sounds like a complete waste of time. Your primary responsibility is to my department, Peter," said Mary. "You're a critical person in this department, and I'll have to speak to the CEO about this and let her know my feelings."*

*Peter left Mary's office deflated and confused. He'd thought this was a great opportunity to break down the silos in the agency and improve communication across the organization. He couldn't understand his boss's reaction.[1]*

We now turn our attention to a model of a new employment relationship. Apart from illustrating a different set of beliefs and expectations, the model is the basis for more constructive dialog between both parties. This collaborative relationship is dependent on a new psychological contract between managers and employees. Without an intentional commitment to open communication, successfully implementing the four proactive strategies I introduce in Chapter 5 won't succeed. As you'll see shortly, the model is diametrically opposite to the traditional model illustrated in the last chapter.

Many organizations are in transition between the old and new psychological contracts. Even within the same organization, these contracts can vary, depending on the leader's expectations and the nature of the work. Nonetheless, the them and us relationship, as I stated, more than anything else, inhibits enterprising employee behavior. I also noted that the transition between the old and new is fraught with confusion and frustration. The new model provides you with some important indicators to assess your progress to forming a collaborative relationship with those you lead. As you read through this chapter, ask yourself this question:

*How closely aligned am I and my team to the new employment relationship model?*

This model, like the traditional employment relationship model, is based on eight shared beliefs. After familiarizing yourself with these beliefs and the expectations supporting theme, in Part II, I explain a new approach to optimize employee empowerment consistent with the new model. This approach, consisting of four strategies, reinforces and strengthens the new psychological contract. The model provides a road-map for fostering the right culture for employee empowerment to thrive.

## New Psychological Contract

I defined what a psychological contract is and what it consists of in the last chapter. This model is like a bookend supporting a shelf of books. We are now moving to the other end of the bookshelf to consider the opposite model. The research-based new employment relationship model illustrates the changing dynamics in the relationship. This new model demonstrates different beliefs and expectations. These two models provide the two ends of the spectrum of the psychological contract.

Also, we discussed some of the factors disrupting the old psychological contract. In previous books, I referred to this as a "workplace revolution" (Baker 2009).[2] This turmoil profoundly disrupted the expectations the employee and employer held of the other. The old and new models serve as reference points to make sense of this shifting employment relationship dynamic.

Table 3.1 illustrates the eight shared beliefs, the matching expectations, and the implications of this new relationship for proactive employee behavior.

You'll notice that the preceding model is formatted identically to Table 2.1 in the previous chapter. It's easier therefore to compare the differences between the two contract models. However, you can see that the eight beliefs, their supporting expectations, and the implications in the new model are diametrically opposite to the traditional model. These polar positions offer a useful framework for understanding the differences between the two psychological contracts. It also serves as a stark

*Table 3.1 New employment relationship model (Baker 2014)[3]*

| Shared belief | Employee's expectation of the manager | Manager's expectation of the employee | Implication for proactive behavior |
|---|---|---|---|
| Flexible deployment | To provide me with opportunities to work in a variety of work settings and contexts | To use your skills and capabilities in a variety of work settings and contexts | A broader range of work experiences promotes proactive behavior |
| Customer focus | To provide me with boundaries to deal with customers and end users | To know the extents and limits of your boundaries when dealing with customers and end users | Boundaries give employees confidence to use their independent judgment in certain situations |
| Performance focus | To communicate to me performance parameters and expectations | To do what needs to be done to get the job done | Clear performance criteria provide the necessary parameters to be proactive |
| Project-based work | To provide me with a clear line of sight between what I do and the desired outcome | To work collaboratively in a variety of teams and work settings | Project work increases the need for independent judgment |
| Human spirit and work | To provide me with meaningful work opportunities | To be engaged in their work | More stimulating work assignments encourage enterprise |
| Commitment | To be appreciated for doing a good job, regardless of my length of tenure | To commit to getting the work done | Showing commitment means that independent judgment is valued |
| Learning and development | To offer me opportunities to grow and develop personally and technically | To be a continuous learner | A culture of learning and development builds autonomous decision-making capabilities |
| Open information | To share with me their vision | To contribute to the team decision-making process | A better-informed employee has the capacity to collaborate in the team decision-making process |

illustration of the dramatic shift required to stimulate useful proactive employee behavior.

The two models are contrasting. These models show the magnitude of the changing employment relationship. It clarifies why there's potential frustration in the relationship and pinpoints when misalignment in beliefs can occur. The juxtaposing of the two models also explains why employee empowerment isn't common practice.

I think it's helpful if I briefly summarize the contrasting beliefs in the two models and their impact on proactive behavior.

## Specialized Employment → Flexible Deployment

*Specialized employment* is the belief that offering clearly defined and specialized employment opportunities is the best way to structure work in a stable and predictable marketplace. Narrow job specifications are easy for management to control; they are also easy for employees to follow. *Flexible deployment*, on the other hand, is a belief that less structured and more adaptable employment opportunities are more suited in a VUCA marketplace. Leaders need to readily deploy people's skill sets to be agile in an ever-changing environment. Employees benefit too, by building a portfolio of capabilities for future career opportunities.

With a broader array of work experiences and with a more expansive deployment of an employee's skills, independent judgment will be expected. However, limited tasks and activities in a clearly defined job role (specialized employment) constraint the need for proactive behavior.

## Internal Focus → Customer Focus

*Internal focus* is making sure that organizational processes and procedures are documented and adhered to. This emphasis is designed to improve organizational efficiency. This strategy is commonly referred to as QA. Like specialized employment, an internal focus enables managerial control. The manager impacts consistent outputs by prescribing the way things are done inside the organization. There is an expectation that the employee will follows these set processes and procedures. While quality assurance is undoubtedly important to success to producing quality products and services, an overreliance on internal quality means the business is less responsive to the ever-changing external environment. A *customer focus*, on the other hand, is concerned with equipping the employee with the necessary resources and information to deal effectively with the customer or end user.

Focusing on the end user, with the manager's support, instills confident in the employee to exercise their independent judgment when the opportunity arises. Customer focus doesn't mean abandoning QA measures, but it does mean balancing internal and external considerations. Since customer requests are more diverse and demanding, the employee needs to use their judgment to deal with this increasing complexity. The end user welcomes resourcefulness when it solves their problem and the business benefits too.

## Job Focus → Performance Focus

A *job focus* is captured in the job description. Under the old contract, the employee fulfills their employment obligations when they fulfill the literal requirements of the job description. Here again, it's about management control. It's easier for the manager to supervise a narrow set of tasks and responsibilities the employee is prescribed to do. Adhering to the requirements of this document is sufficient in a stable and predictable marketplace, where people carry out series of repetitive tasks. *Performance focus*, on the other hand, is concerned with both the job and nonjob requirements. Broadly, a performance focus is doing what needs doing, rather than just following the obligations spelt out in the job description. I discuss these nonjob roles in detail in Chapter 14.

With the rising prominence of nonjob dimension of work, a focus on performance means using independent judgment and displaying initiative.

## Functional-Based Work → Project-Based Work

*Functional-based work* refers to structuring labor in specialized departments. Clustering like-minded jobs together under the same roof has been conventional practice for a century and more. *Project-based work* is structuring labor around projects. Although most businesses are organized around functional roles, most work-related tasks are accomplished cross-functionally. To be able to complete project work, people communicate with other people across departments. Most complex work can be regarded as projects. The problem with functional structures is that jobholders only see a small part of a larger piece of work. This often leads to breakdowns in cross-functional communication. It makes sense therefore to view work as a series of projects rather than functional based.

A project, with its distinctiveness processes and procedures, demands more initiative than working in an organizational silo with its standard operating practices. The global pressures to be more responsive and agile to customer's requests add weight to the argument to shift from functional-based to project-based working arrangements.

## Human Dispirit and Work → Human Spirit and Work

*Human dispirit and work* is associated with jobs that are mundane and narrowly focused. This type of work has little scope for applying independent judgment. Job specification (see Chapter 11), the dominant work design, typically entails completing a limited band of tasks and activities repetitively. These jobs are designed to simplify the training needed (reduces costs) and to minimize error rates (efficiency). Job specification is prevalent across all industries; it's therefore unsurprising that surveys consistently show that more employees are disengaged in their work. *Human spirit and work*, in contrast, is the belief that work—wherever possible—should be designed to be a meaningful experience for the employee.

Work that is stimulating, reasonably challenging, and interesting gives the employee more scope to be creative and exercise their autonomy to problem-solving. This type of work promises to be more engaging. Stimulating work with more variety has the potential to nourish one's human spirit, with opportunities to use their enterprising talents.

## Loyalty → Commitment

*Loyalty* in this context is faithfully adhering to the business's procedures and processes, without questioning its effectiveness. A loyal employee is highly valued in a work setting that is steady and banal. By steadfastly upholding the way things *should* be done, the employee is fulfilling the manager's expectations in the old contract. A loyal employee is likely to stay with the company longer; sometimes too long! Whereas loyalty is a more process driven, *commitment* is more outcome driven.

Committing to achieving business results can involve thinking outside the box. An employee who faithfully follows a business's standard procedures doesn't have right mindset to be enterprising, even when it's useful. On the other hand, committing to getting the work done opens the opportunity to think creatively and question the status quo.

---

# Where the Rubber Meets the Road

### Encouraging Work–Life Balance—Is it All Talk?

Most employers encourage a healthy work–life balance, but they really mean what they say? One leading expert suggests too many companies offer nothing but lip service.

"I have a large amount of cynicism around the sincerity of many companies," states Dr. Linda Duxbery, a management expert. "They talk balance but quite frankly they want people there and they want people working—it's shareholder value, its saving tax-payers' dollars."

According to Duxbery, "We've created a culture of the belief that the dedicated worker, the hard worker, the committed worker is the one who works the long hours and the people who push back are worried about getting ahead or even keeping their job in an environment like the one we have now."

But Duxbery acknowledges that this is probably going to change as millennials begin to make up most of the workforce.

"They put a much higher priority on life," says Duxbery. "They've seen their parents on stress leave, they've seen their parents get divorced, they've seen their parents have drinking problems, on Prozac. They will not stay working for an organization that just gives lip service and doesn't provide balance" (Middlemiss 2015).[4]

## Training → Learning and Development

*Training* emphasizes developing the jobholder's technical skills so they can better fulfill the requirements of their job. Training is primarily focused on improving job skills; it's still the dominant dimension of organizational learning. This hasn't changed in 100 years since the birth of scientific management (see Chapter 14). The main idea of scientific management is that there's *one best way* to do a job.

However, in the last 40 years, we've seen more emphasis placed on personal development and problem-based learning. Job skills' training is still the dominant dimension of organizational learning. *Learning and development* is broader than training and includes the nontechnical aspects of learning. This belief accepts that personal development as an important dimension of employee development.

Personal development and problem-based learning (the two other dimensions of learning and development) assist the employee to be a more confident and skilled decision maker. While training teaches a jobholder how to do a job task, it doesn't usually teach them to use independent judgment.

## Closed Information → Open Information

*Closed information* is providing sufficient information—but no more—for the employee to complete the requirements of their current job. The old saying, *you'll get told on a need-to-know basis* is still heard today in corridors of workplaces, unfortunately. The other common phrase we still hear is *no news is good news*. *Open information* is the opposite. Open information is giving everyone access to a wide range of information beyond that needed to do a job.

Opening the information channels gives the employee a similar perspective to their manager. Having a similar perspective is useful in a dynamic and rapidly changing workplace. A better-informed employee is likely to be more effective; they're more aware of when to seek their manager's input and when to think for themselves. In other words, they know when to bring their thoughts and ideas to the table, when to act autonomously, and to be able to choose between the two.

I hope these descriptors help you to better understand the differences between the two psychological contracts. Although contrasting, identifying the variations in the contracts gives you a more thorough grasp of the changes necessary to build a collaborative working relationship. As I said earlier, the new contract is the cornerstone for promoting proactive employee behavior.

Acting proactively is contingent on the beliefs and expectations managers and employees have of one another. The new employment relationship and its beliefs and expectations cultivate a culture for unleashing employee enterprise. The models provide the two ends of the psychological contract spectrum.

Any human relationship is basically an exchange between people. People's expectations of each other sets the tone for any relationship, personal or work related. The employment relationship is no different to any other relationship. I have illustrated in these two chapters the contrasting beliefs and expectations between the two contracts. These traits shape the interaction between manager and employee.

The shared expectations both parties have of one another reinforce the type of behavior exhibited in the working relationship; it also discourages behaviors that are not consistent with these shared beliefs. In *Breaking the Proactive Paradox*, I want to help you boost employee empowerment. When people's behaviors and expectations are in alignment in the employment relationship, the boundaries of acceptable behavior take shape.

These two models explain the dual responsibilities in the contract. This relationship is formed jointly by satisfying the expectations of the other entity. The first step to forming a new working relationship is understanding the mutual obligations.

If a manager, for instance, doesn't comprehend the changing needs of employees, they'll surely fail to meet their expectations. And if an employee is unfamiliar with the progressive needs of the changing organization, they'll be incapable of carrying out their responsibilities. The new model provides a blueprint for both parties to appreciate what is expected of them. This is the starting point for this collaborative partnership to function properly.

In the next chapter, we look at the proactive paradox model to better appreciate how it undermines employee initiative.

# Top 10 Points

1. Many organizations are in transition between the old and new psychological contracts.

2. Specialized employment is a belief that offering clearly defined and specialized employment opportunities is the best way to structure work in a stable and predictable marketplace. Flexible deployment, on the other hand, is a belief that less structured and more adaptable employment opportunities are more suited to a VUCA marketplace.

3. Internal focus is making sure that organizational processes and procedures are documented and adhered to. A customer focus, on the other hand, is concerned with equipping the employee with the necessary resources and information to deal effectively with the customer or end user.

4. A job focus is captured in the job description. Performance focus, on the other hand, is concerned with both the job and nonjob requirements.

5. Functional-based work refers to structuring labor in specialized departments. Project-based work is structuring labor around projects.

6. Human dispirit and work is associated with jobs that are mundane and narrowly focused. Human spirit and work, in contrast, is the belief that work—wherever possible—should be a meaningful experience for the employee.

7. Loyalty in this context is faithfully adhering to the business's procedures and processes, without questioning it effectiveness. Commitment is more outcomes driven.

8. Training emphasizes developing the jobholder's technical skills so they can better fulfill the requirements of their job. Learning and

development is broader than training and includes the nontechnical aspects of learning.

9. Closed information is providing sufficient information—but no more—so that an employee can complete the requirements of their current job. Open information is giving everyone access to a wide range of information beyond that needed to do a job.

10. These descriptors hopefully help you to understand the obvious difference between the two psychological contracts.

# CHAPTER 4

# The Proactive Paradox Process

*It's ultimately the actions of the manager that speak
louder than the words they speak.*

You now have a better understanding of the psychological contract. We have explored the traditional employment relationship (them and us) in Chapter 2 and the new employment relationship (collaborative) in Chapter 3. You can appreciate that the tallest hurdle in enabling proactive behavior is the traditional contract. The kind of relationship necessary for fostering independent judgment and encouraging initiative is worlds apart from the them and us relationship.

I defined the proactive paradox in Chapter 1. So, now I want to break the paradox down as a process and consider the three key stages and their impact on stifling employee enterprise.

Figure 4.1 shows the proactive paradox process.

As you can see in Figure 4.1, there are three key stages in the proactive paradox process. This paradox, in a nutshell, can be summarized as such: Instead of enabling initiative (something most managers and employees want), the interaction between the manager and employee does the opposite—it stops initiative and entrenches the employee's dependency on their manager. The process, in other words, makes proactive behavior harder, not easier. At the heart of the proactive paradox process—like most problems in the workplace—is a breakdown in communication.

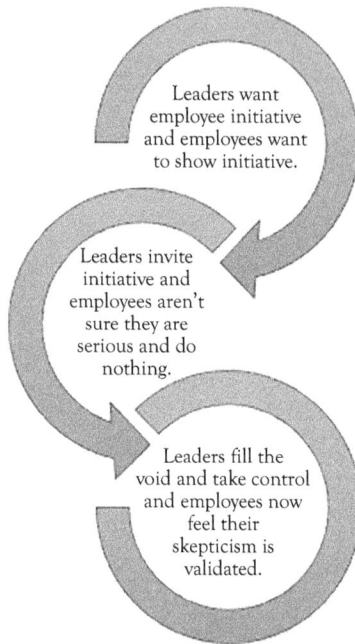

*Figure 4.1 Proactive paradox process*

---

## Where the rubber meets the road

### What's a paradox?

A paradox is a statement or problem that either appears to produce two entirely contradictory (yet possible) outcomes or provides proof for something that goes against what we intuitively expect. Paradoxes have been a central part of philosophical thinking for centuries. They are always ready to challenge our interpretation of otherwise simple situations, turning what we might think to be true on its head and presenting us with provably plausible situations that are in fact just as provably impossible. Confused? You should be.

Imagine you're holding a postcard in your hand, on one side of which is written, "The statement on the other side of this card is true." We'll call that Statement A. Turn the card over, and the opposite side reads, "The statement on the other side of this card is false" (Statement

B). Trying to assign any truth to either Statement A or B, however, leads to a paradox: if A is true, then B must be as well, but for B to be true, A must be false. Oppositely, if A is false, then B must be false too, which must ultimately make A true (Jones 2016).[1]

Let's consider the three stages illustrated in Figure 4.1. They can be labelled as follows:

- Agreement
- Skepticism
- Confirmation

## Agreement

In general, under the new psychological contract, the manager and employee are on the same page regarding the value of proactive behavior. The leader wants team members to act proactively when and where necessary. For example, it there is a problem, they want the person involved to go ahead and fix it (if possible). Leaders want team members to speak up in meetings when they have something worthwhile to contribute. They want them to ask questions if they don't understand something, and so on. Team members also for the most part want to act proactively in the right place at the right time. For example, they don't want to check-in with their leader every time they make a decision. Some do of course, but they embrace the values of the old contract. Employees generally want to contribute to meetings and offer suggestions. They want to be clear about what they are doing in their work and feel comfortable asking questions to seek out clarification. There is overall agreement between leader and team member.

Even with a general understanding about importance of proactive behavior, there will inevitably be disparities in expectations between a manager and employee. These differences add a layer of complexity to what would seem like a simple agreement. It's not just *what* initiative is important and unimportant, but *when* it should and shouldn't be displayed, and *how* it's to be done. A manager's tolerance of proactive behavior is also depending on *who* it is that is displaying it. So, there are a range of factors that influence a manager's acceptance of employee initiative, despite a general feeling that proactivity in positive.

Although most employees want to use their independent judgment to some extent, they too have differing expectations. At its most basic, some employees want more direction from their manager and others want more freedom and autonomy. The continuum ranges from employees wanting complete independence to the manager being totally hands-on. Employees also fluctuate in their need for autonomy and dependence, based on the type of challenge they face. Notwithstanding the prevailing psychological contract, each employee has their own set of beliefs about taking responsibility and being accountable for acting proactively.

Unsurprisingly, these variances in expectation between leaders and team members lead to discord. Aside from these factors I've outlined, disappointment boils down to a simple proposition: Either the manager is frustrated with an employee, who they think isn't proactive enough, or the employee is frustrated with the manager because they believe they are muzzled their autonomy. In other words, the manager is critical of the employee for lacking resourcefulness or being too dependent on them. Or the employee is critical of the manager for being too controlling and not allowing them to exercise enough independence. It all boils down to the degree of managerial control and the willingness for the employee to be a self-starter.

Although the psychological contract generally contributes to expressing or suppressing proactive behavior, individual preferences have a role to play too. This friction is likely to be more pronounced in the transition between the old and new contract, where expectations are fuzzy and not congruent between the manager and employee. This tension may occur notwithstanding the overall belief that being proactive is desirable behavior in the mind of most managers and employees. Good communication practices can remedy these differences. We consider four strategies in Part II.

Most managers, however, typically think their team members could be more enterprising. Leaders form these views from their observations of incidents in the workplace. Team members also form their views of managers by watching them deal with situations at work. I'll demonstrate the proactive paradox process and its three stages by observing the interactions between Felicity (leader) and Jeremy (team member). Their simple interactions illustrate how these perceptions are formed, the generalizations that are made, and its negative bearing on proactive behavior:

Felicity observes Jeremy not following up accounts to get the latest figures to formulate a budget for the new financial year. Although Felicity is responsible for the overall budget, Jeremy is expected to formulate the budget in the first place. *Why didn't he act? What is stopping him?* Felicity asks herself. Instead, she sees Jeremy coming to her complaining that accounts have not furnished the team with the latest update. Jeremy seems to think that Felicity should get involved in this matter.

Felicity is quietly irritated. She interprets this situation as a signal that Jeremy doesn't want to take responsibility or—is he covering their backside in case something goes wrong? Felicity is mildly upset with Jeremy for not following this up himself.

But instead of sending Jeremy away and asking him to follow up accounts, she makes the mistake of contacting accounts herself. Felicity rationalizes that it's quicker this way. Perhaps next time Jeremy will think first. Big mistake.

Jeremy has a different perception. He believes Felicity expects to be informed about this situation. Ironically, Jeremy feels a little upset too. He wants to be more autonomy in his role. But because of a lack of clarity, Jeremy isn't sure how and when to use independent judgment. Observing that when he raises this matter with Felicity and she immediately follows up accounts, Jeremy assumes she sees this as her responsibility, rather than his. He thinks that maybe Felicity doesn't want him to act on his own.

When a team member asks their manager a question and they respond by answering it immediately, or jumps in and solves a problem, the employee is quite capable of answering, they naturally assume their manager prefers it this way. Furthermore, the team member believes that because they aren't told to work it out themselves, the manager wants to do it themselves.

Jeremy thinks that Felicity wants him to bring her this problem (and probably other problems) to solve. *Perhaps Felicity doesn't want me to show any initiative? Perhaps my job is to keep Felicity informed and up to date? This is how she wants our working relationship to be.*

The first of several misunderstandings arises in the proactive paradox process; that is, though the employee is capable and willing to solve their own challenges, the manager wants to deal with their problems and issues. And the manager may doubt that the employee wants to *own* the problem.

A simple interaction like this raises doubts in the mind of the employee:

- Why do I have to check-in all the time with the boss?
- Why can't they trust me and allow me to back myself?
- The boss has given me the answers; doesn't she want me to think for myself?

Jeremy assumes that in the future he should just check-in with Felicity and not go out on a limb and think for himself. *Play the game and making sure I curb my initiative; this is the best way to stay out of trouble*, thinks Jeremy.

The employee observes some incidents of micromanagement from their manager and feels they have little or no room to move. This is just the way it is, the employee concedes.

Felicity attends a leadership program. Jacky, her manager, sends her to the course to learn to "let go" and not micromanage, having observed a few incidents. Throughout the program, the trainer reminds Felicity that employees who display their initiative and act with enterprise tend to have higher levels of engagement.

Several strategies are suggested in the training program to encourage more proactive behavior. Returning to work with some hope and optimism, Felicity commits to building this enterprising environment so that engagement can flourish in her team. She is all for getting her team to think independently.

With this compelling and straightforward message, Felicity thinks her team needs to know that they have her *permission* to be proactive. She commits to communicating this message at the next team meeting. If I make my intentions clearer, perhaps employees will be more proactive, Felicity believes.

At the next team meeting, Felicity urges their team members to act with initiative. Without specifics, this is the message conveyed at the meeting. That was easy. All I need to do now, she thinks, is sit back and wait for the team to be respond.

But of course, it isn't that simple; it never is. This is when Felicity and Jeremy move to the second stage in the proactive paradox process: *skepticism.*

## Skepticism

After Felicity's big announcement at the team meeting, the room goes silent. Her team is skeptical. Team members aren't convinced that Felicity really wants them to be proactive, least of all, Jeremy! They've seen no evidence to suggest this is what she really wants.

When managers make these announcements, they assume the message has hit the mark.

Felicity's team do the opposite to what they've been asked to do. They play it safe and decide to continue with what they have been doing: not being proactive. Instead, they continue relying on Felicity for advice, to respond to their questions, and give them direction. Surely, *this is what she really wants and expects?* they think.

This raises two important questions at this stage of the process:

- Why has the message of the manager not cut through?
- Why don't the team think their manager is serious?

Leaders often urge their team members to act on their independent judgment, without giving them any guidelines. But team members are not, understandably, convinced—they aren't too sure whether the leader genuinely wants them acting in enterprising ways. Employees are often skeptical because the manager's behavior and rhetoric don't match. When there's a mismatch in what they say and what they do, the safest option is to carry on doing what they have always done. This means that the employee continues to rely on their leader to give them direction. Instead of being proactive, they remain reactive.

Although Jeremy and his colleagues heard Felicity *direct* them to be more proactive, they doesn't buy it. There's too much conflicting evidence. After all, Jeremy surmises, *if Felicity really meant that, why does she take charge whenever I approached her with a possible solution? Why was she so forthright with her response to my question?* There is an abundance of illustrations I have seen to suggest that what Felicity said is not what she means.

The employee justifies that if the boss really means what they say, they would have got out of the way and allowed them to exercise their initiative. It's just words. Besides, the employee recalls at least one occasion when they did take initiative. They were reprimanded for not keeping the manager informed, even though it seemed completely unnecessary. From that point on, the team member decides to be cautious and checks with the boss before making a move. Better to be safe than sorry.

Although the employee would rather be proactive, they're reactive instead, in the interests of self-preservation. Being reactive seems less risky than behaving proactively. Remaining unconvinced, nothing changes. Given a choice between following a set process and acting proactively, the safer option is to follow the system. By doing things by the book, they can back themselves by stating that they were simply following due process.

The irony is obvious: If the employee were genuinely encouraged to be proactive, they would be because they want to be.

## Confirmation

Now at this stage of the proactive paradox process, things get interesting. This is a pivotal moment:

> Felicity despairingly observes the continuation of this reactive behavior. Nothing changes. After communicating that she wants people to be more proactive, Felicity's incorrect conclusion is that team members don't really want to be proactive. Her frustration is amplified with this persistent lack of enterprise. This passive response to Felicity's *encouragement* to be more proactive results in her rushing in and being more directive and autocratic than she intended. She feels the need to fill the void. Felicity is now *convinced* that her team members are incapable of being proactive, despite her best *efforts* to advocate it.

More distrust creeps into the already tense employment relationship. On one hand, the team member doesn't trust the leader to step back and allow them to exercise their autonomy. On the other hand, the manager doesn't trust the team member to show the necessary initiative needed to do the job. This standoff solidifies the misbehavior of both parties. The employee consequently continues to be cautious, observing this more autocratic behavior from their manager. The manager notices this reticence to be proactive and decides to be more directive, rationalizing that if they don't, nothing will get done. And both parties are entrenched in their behavior and annoyed with the other for their behavior!

In this predicament, the manager overestimates the effort they have put in to encouraging proactive employee behavior. Simultaneously, they underestimate their own behavior in discouraging initiative.

> With a lack of trust borne out of frustration, Felicity doesn't receive any feedback to suggest she is on the wrong track, except

to be sent on a leadership training program by Jacky. She never explained why Felicity was sent on the course.

Creating the right environment to encourage initiative takes more than the odd proclamation about the value and importance of employee enterprise. These words—as well meaning as they are intended—are just words. It's ultimately the actions of the manager that speak louder than the words they speak. Some of these actions that accompany the manager's rhetoric offer subtle hints. It could be as simple as a raised eyebrow when an employee mentions that they had taken the initiative in an area. Or, it could be more blatant, such as chastising the employee for not keeping them well informed. At any rate, it is the behavior that's problematic, not the words. The correct behavior sets the tone.

When rhetoric doesn't match reality, it's the reality that wins out. Employees are more attuned to what the manager does, rather than what they say, in other words. Managers need to be more reflective and self-aware to understand the negative impressions they convey by their actions.

But at this stage in the proactive paradox process, the employee observes the manager continuing to intrude in areas they feel they should be responsible for, despite their words. The employee has balked at being proactive; they haven't seen enough evidence to indicate a change in attitude. What's more, they observe that the manager is even more strident about jumping in. This reinforces the original feeling that the manager wasn't really serious about the employee exhibiting proactive behavior. Simultaneously, it strengthens the employee's attitude that being reactive is expected. Even so, both parties wanted it the other way round. It's a paradox.

Jeremy observing Felicity interfering and making decisions that she has asked him to make. It now seems obvious to Jeremy that Felicity was never serious about him being proactive. This sequence of stages discourages him from being proactive even further. It confirms Jeremy's view.

Team members observe what they interpret as micromanaging from their leader. This directive leadership behavior validates the team member's initial skepticism. The team member assumes, in other words, that they were right in their original judgment; that is, management wasn't really serious about displays of initiative. And now, it's the employees' turn to feel frustration. So, the proactive paradox is based on misunderstandings—and the reinforcement of these misunderstandings—about the motives of the other party in the employment relationship.

This process has made things worse, not better. The manager is more annoyed than they were at the outset. They are upset that the employee is incapable and unwilling to exercise any enterprise. They give up on the idea of empowering employees to make decisions.

Employees are just as exasperated. They have given up on the idea of showing any independent judgment. It seems pointless. The manager, regardless of what they say, doesn't want proactive behavior from their team members.

This is the proactive paradox and how it plays out.

We are at the end of Part I. My purpose here was to explain the proactive paradox and the manager–employee relationship as a barrier to reinforcing it. In Part II, we look at a new approach to minimize this contradiction.

# Top 10 Points

1. Instead of enabling initiative (something most managers and employees want), the interaction between the manager and employee does the opposite—it stops initiative and entrenches the employee's dependency on their manager.

2. The proactive paradox process has three stages: agreement, skepticism, and confirmation.

3. In general, under the new psychological contract, the manager and employee are on the same page regarding the value of proactive behavior.

4. Even with a general understanding about importance of proactive behavior, there will inevitably be disparities in expectations between a manager and employee.

5. These differences add a layer of complexity to what would seem like agreement.

6. The first of several misunderstandings arises in the proactive paradox process; that is, though the employee is capable and willing to solve their own challenges, the manager wants to deal with their problems and issues.

7. Leaders often urge their team members to act on their independent judgment, without giving them any guidelines.

8. In the confirmation stage, the team member doesn't trust the manager to step back and allow them to exercise their autonomy. And the manager doesn't trust the team member to show the necessary initiative needed to do the job.

9. In this predicament, the manager overestimates the effort they have put in to encouraging proactive employee behavior. Simultaneously, they underestimate their own behavior in discouraging initiative.

10. Creating the right environment to encourage initiative takes more than the odd proclamation about the value and importance of employee enterprise.

PART II

# Strategies for Resolving the Paradox

# CHAPTER 5

# The Four Strategies

How does a leader encourage team members to use independent judgment when it's required? And simultaneously, how does a leader ensure the same people follow company guidelines and processes when needed?

*Rachel received a phone call from an irate customer. "Your last invoice overcharged me on my telephone bill by $149.90. I'm not happy about this and want it fixed straight away!" demanded Charlie Robertson.*

*"Okay Mr. Robertson let me bring up your account details on my screen; I won't be a moment," replied an anxious Rachel.*

*"Yes, there appears to be a mistake Mr. Robertson, according to our records. I'll need to talk to my manager about this and get back to you."*

*"Why do you need to talk to your boss if it's obvious that you have made a mistake in your billing?" demanded Charlie, in an intimidating tone.*

*"That's company policy Mr. Robertson."*

*Once off the phone, Rachel immediately went to speak with Maryanne, her manager about Mr. Robertson's situation. Maryanne looked at Rachel and said, after momentarily studying the information on the screen of her computer, "Obviously there is an error. Call Mr. Robertson back immediately and let him know that we'll credit him this amount in our next invoice."*

*Just as Rachel was about to leave her manager's office, Maryanne said, "Okay, let's set a rule here, Rachel. From now on, if a customer calls and complains, and it's obvious that we have made an error and it involves a sum of $200 or less, then I want you to fix it straight away without consulting me. That way, we're unlikely to antagonize the* *customer any more than necessary. I want you to show initiative in future under these circumstances; okay?"*

*Rachel called the customer back to reassure him. Charlie Robertson responded with, "Thank you, but I don't understand why you needed to talk to your manager if the situation was obviously a mistake."*

*Rachel felt a little more empowered now, knowing that her boss wanted her to show initiative if a billing error in future was less than $200. Although feeling more confident, Rachel hoped that this kind of error wouldn't occur again.*

In Part I, we discussed the origins of the proactive paradox and the barriers the manager–employee relationship can create. The world of work is generally in transition between the traditional and new psychological contracts. This shift makes employee enterprise even more challenging. The old them and us relationship has a simple separation of responsibilities between the manager and employee. But as this traditional psychological contract is unravelling, it creates confusion around boundaries and expectations. For instance, an employee may still embrace the beliefs of the old contract and their manager may accept the new contract and vice versa. *Breaking the Proactive Paradox* offers a new framework consisting of four strategies designed to minimize the uncertainty around when and where enterprising behavior starts and finishes.

Part II discusses these four broad strategies and how they can be applied.

As you can appreciate from the proactive paradox process we covered in the last chapter, empowering employees to make enterprising decisions is more complex than it seems. Enterprise is, nonetheless, the cornerstone of agile performance that's needed today. Resolving this proactive paradox is crucial for success. There are now more employees and managers working across more industry groups than ever before. Apart from affecting more people—if the Covid-19 pandemic teaches us anything—it's the pressing need to be agile to address the unanticipated challenges of our time. In essence, the proactive paradox is caused by miscommunication (or no communication) between the leader and team member.

## Where the Rubber Meets the Road

### The Tranny of Head Office

Consider a retail franchise business. Employees will often talk about *ownership* when they refer to their involvement in a retail outlet. The shop bound employee is no doubt multiskilled or flexibly deployed in all the tasks and activities of running the retail operation. This same employee typically questions what they think is needless interference by head office in the running of *their* store. This "intrusion" may involve such things as policy making, customer interaction, purchasing, stock control, and implementing new systems and procedures. Head office's involvement often causes tension in the retail outlets.

Based on head office input, the employee in the store assumes that their initiative to make decisions is being sabotaged. And because they think there's unnecessary interference in their day-to-day store operations, they're less inclined to be proactive. Management observes this lack of resourcefulness; they assume that employees in the stores can't, or won't, act with initiative when needed. Head office becomes irritated with frontline employees, whom they think are too reliant upon management to make simple operational decisions. So, management reluctantly feels justified to make decisions in operational matters. This vicious cycle leads to negative feelings all round.

Better communication channels equip employees to be many things:

- More knowledgeable
- More self-sufficient
- More participative
- More adaptive
- More flexible
- More efficient
- More responsive

For most managers and employees, clearer communication is appealing, but it's not well practiced.

The crux of the problem is: *How does a leader encourage team members to use independent judgment when it's required? And simultaneously, how does a leader ensure the same people follow company guidelines and processes when needed?* Managers have tried an assortment of tactics to resolve this dilemma. Company rules have been introduced. Workplaces regulated. Policies formulated. And guidelines proposed. Some tools have worked, but most have failed.

I'm sure you can think of examples of too much autonomy leading to disaster—or more likely on other occasions—a lack of employee enterprise causing problems. Getting the balance of too little and too much initiative is challenging. I'm sure you'd agree with me.

So, how's this paradox broken?

Here are four strategies to stimulate and regulate independent judgment. These strategies open the lines of communication to clarify when proactive behavior is acceptable and unacceptable:

- Shared purpose
- Boundary management
- Information exchange
- Proactive accountability

Let's define each strategy.

## Shared Purpose

The strategy of *shared purpose* aligns the perspectives of team members and leader in a common direction. If a team member isn't on the same page as their leader and decide to act proactively, this can be a problem. The leader will reject this initiative if it isn't consistent with their view. If a team member and leader share the same purpose, however, using prudent initiative to achieve it will probably be appreciated by the leader. When there's agreement between the objectives of the two parties, the team member feels confident about using their own judgment.

Without a shared purpose, enterprising behavior will be curtailed, usually after a clash with management for what they perceive as misguided action. Independent judgment is curbed in future. Once bitten, twice shy.

The assumption supporting shared purpose is that when there's agreement between the leader and team member on the goals of the work unit, this encourages appropriate proactive behavior.

A misalignment of purpose, on the other hand, causes confusion and conflict. Take, for instance, a company that espouses *transparency* and *honesty* as their core values. If the senior executive team holds lots of secretive meetings behind closed doors and information from these meetings is withheld from employees, this sends a contradictory message. Furthermore, these closed-door meetings infer that management relationships are fractured, and this suggests low trust. Employees are hardly likely to be practiced transparency and honesty after witnessing this dysfunctional behavior. Worse still, it's possible this example with have the opposite affect; that is, secrecy and untruthfulness may surge well beyond the boardroom. At any rate, there's complete discord between what is espoused (the values) and what is practiced (the secret meetings).

One of the simplest—yet most neglected—ways of creating a shared purpose is for leaders to "walk the talk." If the members of the executive team consistently demonstrate transparency and honesty in their dealings with each other, the rest of the organization will most probably follow suit. Alignment between values and behavior at the senior level will probably permeate throughout the rest of the business.

Here's another illustration of misalignment of purpose: Samantha sends a mixed signal during a casual discussion with Dominic, one of her team members. She insists that Dominic keep her well informed about all his interactions with a difficult customer. At the same time, Samantha tells Dominic to use his common sense and show initiative with this customer, when he needs to. When told later about Dominic's proactive approach with this customer, Samantha chastises him for taking that action. This criticism understandably confuses Dominic. If Samantha criticizes his actions without first praising him for using his judgment, he'll justifiably interprets this as criticism for being proactive. The outcome is confusion, not shared purpose, the opposite of what Samantha wants. Dominic puts his cue in the rack after this unpleasant encounter with Samantha.

In Chapter 7, we explore some practical measures to promote shared purpose.

## Boundary Management

A second way of breaking the proactive paradox is *boundary management*. This strategy involves communicating the kind of initiative the leader wants—and doesn't want. In other words, boundary management is communicating the extent and limits of an individual's authority to be enterprising in their work. Explaining when and where enterprising behavior is welcome and unwelcome clarifies the boundaries for proactive behavior. Not communicating these boundaries, on the other hand, results in ambiguity. A team member will understandably be confused and hesitant about using their independent judgment.

The assumption underpinning this strategy is that in certain situations, it's appropriate and expected that independent judgment be used. But in other circumstances, it's inappropriate to use one's initiative.

Given the complexities of organizational life, boundary management is easier to suggest than to accomplish. Nonetheless, when a team member is confused about when or where to apply their own judgment, it's usually because their leader hasn't clarified the boundaries. In practice, boundary management is a never-ending dialog between leader and team member.

Boundary management needs to be an ongoing conversation because task requirements and situations continually change; they change over time, sometimes rapidly without warning. Although boundaries can change, a leader who is aware of these changes can sometimes anticipate them. The essence of boundary management is to immediately communicate a change in expectations when a novel circumstance arises. Constant dialog builds trust and instils confidence in team members to act (or not act) proactively.

Apart from regular conversations, an effective leader uses a variety of other tactics to communicate inevitable boundary shifts. Team meetings, critical incident debriefs, coaching, e-mail, and written instructions are some of the main methods for communicating changes.

Here is an illustration, combining two approaches: a team meeting and critical incident. Consider a common dilemma facing an airline company: An incident where an airplane has been grounded with unfore-seen mechanical difficulties. What are the roles and responsibilities of airline personnel when this scenario occurs? To clarify and communicate the appropriate boundaries in this predicament, a leader can organize a series of meetings to debrief on a recent aircraft grounding incident. The debriefings may comprise a cross-section of the company, including pilots, flight attendants, engineers, customer service representatives, sales-people, and operational crew.

In discussing this scenario, the focus is to clarify functional boundar-ies and responsibilities when a similar incident occurs. In other words, the meetings are designed to explain and appreciate each person's role, where and when it is permissible to act using independent judgment, and when it's not. The overriding consideration is how each functional area com-municates and acts to minimize passenger inconvenience, while ensur-ing safety standards are upheld. The aim is getting the plane airborne as quickly as possible, without compromising safety standards.

By discussing this incident together in a meeting, it enables team mem-bers to elucidate when and where they should perform to resolve this com-mon, but unfortunate scenario. This exercise is likely to generate awareness and confidence to act proactively when similar situations arise. And it also defines when to follow procedures and not use independent judgment.

Boundary management confines employee initiative to specific areas of their role. This strategy also clarifies when and where proactive behavior is not warranted. Boundary management will appeal to the team member who's tentative about exercising independent judgment and the leader who's cautious about giving employees free rein. This strategy regulates proactive behavior.

A leader who feels uncomfortable relying too heavily on people's independent judgment can use boundary management to restrain certain types of proactive behavior. The team member who is cautious about dis-playing their initiative will find this strategy appealing too.

Although boundary management will be less appealing to a leader wanting an expansive use of independent judgment, the team member who is eager to work autonomously in their role will find boundary man-agement somewhat restrictive because it's their leader who decides where these boundaries start and finish.

In Chapter 8, I have explained some ways you can use boundary management.

# Information Exchange

*Information exchange* builds trust and aligns the leader and team member's perspective, like the shared purpose strategy. But there's a difference. Information exchange gives team members more scope to be involved in decision making than shared purpose, where the purpose is determined by the manager. With information exchange, the team and their leader collaborate—decisions on direction, goals, and decisions are made jointly. Information exchange concentrates on minimizing differences in viewpoint by exchanging ideas.

This collaboration is done by opening the channels of communication to everyone in the team, regardless of their hierarchical status. By providing everyone working in the team with the same information, mutual understanding is cocreated.

The basic assumption in this approach is that by building trust through collaboration and partnership, everyone gains a similar outlook on a range of important business matters.

This strategy supports enterprising behavior from a steady flow of information between the leader and the team. Employees are considered partners, not subordinates. Information exchange is particularly useful in strategic planning and business improvement.

Here is an illustration: Bob hired a professional facilitator for his team's annual retreat. The purpose of Bob's retreat is to develop, evaluate, and modify his team's strategic direction and purpose together as a team. This meeting is an opportunity to share ideas. Bob begins the retreat by explaining the rationale of the retreat, inviting the whole team to actively participate. During the retreat, the facilitator works with the team to develop a structured team plan, engaging everyone in the room. The retreat is a success. Bob's team comes away with series of strategies, plans-of-action, accountabilities, and timelines to meet several goals over the coming year.

He always gets great value from these retreats; the information exchange process enables his team to speak a common language.

This mutual understanding instills confidence in Bob's team members to take the necessary initiative where and when needed to achieve their collective goals and milestones.

Information exchange can be used to improve the team's efficiency and effectiveness in other ways. For example, Allison invites her team to explore ways and means of developing the team's processes. She invites her team to identify one area that needs improving within the team's span-of-influence. This exercise aims to do things faster, easier, safer, with better quality, or improved communication.

After some thought, several issues are put on the table for consideration. Allison then invites her team to vote on the issue they believe to be the most pressing or relevant. Through consensus, the team decides their number one improvement priority is minimizing the time spent on e-mail communication. Her team then gets to work on this priority. An e-mail protocol is developed. With the free exchange of ideas, everyone in Allison's team commits to the plan to improve the way they communicate via e-mail.

In these two examples, Bob and Allison are essentially sharing their managerial role with members of their team. Team members gain a better insight into their manager's thinking on important issues, procedures, and priorities. Leaders also gain a clearer understanding of the views of their team members. For information exchange to work, the leader must openly shares work unit information with colleagues and encourages team members to reciprocate by freely sharing their points-of-view.

Such frankness exposes the leader somewhat. Furthermore, the leader becomes more reliant on their team to share the leadership. Information exchange elevates trust levels between the leader and team and between team members. This is a positive outcome that inevitably encourages employees to exercise their enterprising qualities.

In Chapter 9, we explore some practical tools to implement information exchange.

## Proactive Accountability

*Proactive accountability* is based on an understanding that initiative and independent judgment are permissible in certain cases, but the initiator is ultimately accountable for the outcome, not the manager. If the outcome of displaying independent judgment is unacceptable to management, this can have negative consequences for the employee who initiated the action. The risk of proactive behavior, in other words, is carried by the employee.

This strategy is characteristic of bureaucratic and authority-focused workplaces, such as military and paramilitary organizations. These work environments usually have a clearly defined chain-of-command for decision making.

The assumption supporting proactive accountability is that there is room for initiative and independent judgment, but the initiator is ultimately accountable for their own proactive actions.

Consider Marco; he's in-charge of purchasing stock in a large corporation with very stringent purchasing rules and regulations. One of the company's policies is to order stock in the last week of the month. But Marco has advance notice that his company has won a large contract with a big customer. This customer requires immediate delivery of the product. It's the beginning of the month. Marco decides to place the order early in the month in respond to the immediate needs of the customer. This enterprising behavior violates a major company policy. But by taking this initiative, Marco delights the customer with quick responsiveness; and management isn't critical of Marco for his enterprise.

Here's another example in a military environment.

Max, a squadron leader, refuses to comply with an illegal order from Joe, his direct superior. Specifically, Joe orders Max to cover up the details of a murder before the official investigation takes place. By not following orders, Max has violating a command from his superior officer. While the subordinate may suffer initially for insubordination from his commanding officer, Max doesn't undergo negative consequences outside the confines of the military unit. Officers beyond Joe's command are supportive of Max's stance on this potential cover-up.

In these two examples, the organization allows employees to use their independent judgment, but only on the basis that management may treat an error of judgment harshly. On the other hand, although the risk resides with the initiator, a successful outcome is acceptable.

As you probably realize, proactive accountability is the least effective of the four strategies for fostering employee initiative. This strategy does, however, have its place in a framework of regulating and restricting proactive behavior. Proactive accountability is different from the other three strategies in that it doesn't clearly specify the conditions when initiative should take place. Yet this strategy acknowledges that exceptional circumstances—such as the examples we discussed—may benefit from independent judgment and that there is a time and place to bend the rules.

Uncertainty around whether to go against or follow the rules means an employee will at least hesitate before taking proactive action. And if their subsequent actions cause a problem, proactive accountability ends with the leader being free of any accountable for their team member's actions. By applying this strategy, the leader can place the responsibility with the proactive person on the grounds they didn't follow the rules and protocol. The employee is ultimately accountable for any misjudgment. So, the employee can't be certain the organization will back their judgment and subsequent actions.

Proactive accountability is assessed dynamically. Managerial judgment is done case-by-case, in other words, with the benefit of hindsight. Any benefits from this strategy are heavily in favor of the organization rather than the individual. There are few pluses for the proactive employee, especially when poor judgment is exercised! Apart from bureaucratic organizations, this strategy suits the traditional psychological contract, where the manager is expected to have all the decision-making authority. However, it does—in special circumstances—have application in the new contract. Though proactive accountability will discourage—not encourage—enterprising behavior overall.

In Chapter 10, I share some circumstances where proactive accountability can be applied and how it can be managed.

By using these four strategies, the leader can overcome two significant roadblocks in breaking the proactive paradox. The first barrier is enticing employees to make autonomous decisions. The second roadblock is knowing where and when to use independent judgment. Having a framework that guides the use of different forms of initiative (and compliance) is beneficial to both the leader and team member. The four strategies can be used separately or in combinations. The proactive framework is a useful way to regulate and restrain independent judgment.

In the next chapter, we consider the proactive framework and its application.

# Top 10 Points

1. Better communication channels equip employees to be more knowledgeable, self-sufficient, participative, adaptive, flexible, efficient, and responsive.
2. The strategy of shared purpose aligns the perspectives of team members and leaders in a common direction.
3. The assumption supporting shared purpose is that when there's agreement between the leader and team member on the goals of the work unit, this encourages appropriate proactive behavior.
4. Boundary management involves communicating the kind of initiative the leader wants and doesn't want.
5. The assumption underpinning boundary management is that in certain situations, it's appropriate and expected that independent judgment be used. But in other situations, it's inappropriate to use one's initiative.
6. Information exchange builds trust and aligns the leader and team member's perspective, like the shared purpose strategy.
7. The basic assumption of information exchange is that by building trust through collaboration and partnership, everyone gains a similar outlook on a range of important business matters.
8. Proactive accountability is based on an understanding that initiative and independent judgment are permissible in certain cases, but the initiator is ultimately accountable for the outcome, not the manager.
9. The assumption supporting proactive accountability is that there is room for initiative and independent judgment, but the initiator is ultimately accountable for their own proactive actions.
10. By using these four strategies, the leader can overcome two significant roadblocks in breaking the proactive paradox.

# CHAPTER 6

# The Proactive Framework

*… a proactive employee isn't a commodity to be purchased via a recruitment and selection process.*

*"These three employees have demonstrated outstanding loyalty to our company," claimed Jim. "They've been working here for 25 years. I think we should reward them at the Christmas Party."*
*"What did you have in mind, Jim?" asked Chris, Jim's boss.*

*"I thought we should buy them a flat-screen plasma TV and present it to them at party. What do you think?"*

*Chris looked at Jim pensively and paused. "What signal will this send the troops, Jim?" "It'll send a signal to staff that we value them—we care about them. It demonstrates that we value loyalty."*

*There was a long pause and Chris asked, "What about commitment? Does it show that we value commitment?" "What do you mean, Chris? Aren't they the same thing—loyalty and commitment?" Jim asked with a puzzled look.*

*"No, I don't think so. You can be loyal without being committed and committed without being loyal." "What do you mean?"*

*"You have a university degree, don't you Jim?" "Yes, I do." "Well, you must have shown a certain level of commitment to complete that qualification, right. But that doesn't mean you there is a long-term loyalty to the university that issued you with the qualification, does it?" "I guess not," replied Jim.*

*"Similarly, a university student can be loyal to a partner in a short-term relationship, but that doesn't mean there is a long-term commitment for life."*

*"Remember this Jim, the only rats that leave a sinking ship are the ones that can swim. Sometimes we don't want or need people to stay with the company for a long time. It's what people do that's important, not how long people decide to stay."*

*After another long pause, Jim poses the question, "Should we be rewarding loyalty or commitment?"*

*"I'm not against recognizing these three employees for their length of service. But I think we should balance this by recognizing those employees who are committed to assisting our company achieve its business goals."*

*"Okay, I get the point. I'll rethink this and get back to you"* (Baker 2017).[1]

Each of the four strategies we covered in the previous chapter is designed to either enable or curb undesirable proactive behavior, or both.

Boundary management and proactive accountability are strategies to confine enterprising behavior to specific situations and circumstances. The role of the leader applying boundary management is to identify and communicate appropriate and inappropriate conditions for exercising independent judgment. Proactive accountability restrains proactive behavior by making it clear to employees that they are ultimately responsible for the outcome of their enterprising behavior. If employee initiative is exercised using this strategy, its outcome will determine whether their action is acceptable or unacceptable. If independent judgment proves to be the right course-of-action, then there're no negative consequences for the initiator, apart from the possible circumstances leading to their actions. But if the behavior is viewed adversely, it will probably lead to undesirable results for the employee. Put simply, proactive accountability means: You are welcome to show initiative at your own risk.

Shared purpose and information exchange invite suitable initiative by fostering a common understanding, similar perspective, and clear expectations. An alignment of viewpoints between employee and manager is the desired outcome of shared purpose. This similar point-of-view assumes the employee will feel safe to be proactive in pursuit of a commonly held outcome. Information exchange is a strategy where the employee and manager collaborate based on a common understanding. Working as partners maximizes a shared expectancy and minimizes the likelihood of undesirable independent judgment being exercised. Consequently, if shared purpose and information exchange are well executed, unwelcomed proactive behavior is apparent to everyone. But the primary aim of shared purpose and information exchange is to promote proactive behavior in the right place and at the right time.

To better illustrate these distinctions, the four-strategy framework is illustrated in the following.

*Table 6.1  The proactive framework*

| Stimulating proactivity | Regulating proactivity | |
| --- | --- | --- |
| Shared purpose | Boundary management | **Manager initiated** |
| Information exchange | Proactive accountability | **Employee initiated** |

The proactive framework has two dimensions: *stimulating* or *regulating proactivity* and *manager* or *employee initiated*. Let's define these parameters first before discussing some implications of their use.

Stimulating proactivity emphasizes encouraging over limiting proactive behavior. This doesn't mean that all independent judgment is appropriate, of course. Apart from stimulating proactivity, the two strategies in the left-hand column are designed to reduce the uncertainty of when to use independent judgment. Confidence is built by aligning perspectives and expectations. If both share a similar outlook, it promises that the employee will feel more comfortable making independent decisions. They are also less likely to exhibit unwarranted initiative.

Regulating proactivity has a different emphasis. This orientation focuses more on discouraging unsuitable proactive behavior over inspiring it. These two strategies in the right-hand column therefore entail clarifying the limits of proactive behavior. By communicating the parameters of enterprise, the manager is containing independent judgment to certain situations.

Now we look at the horizontal dimension. Manager initiated (top row) involves the leader providing the impetus. With management guidance, it's apparent to the employee where their enterprising qualities are needed (and undesirable). For these two strategies, the manager makes the first move, defining the limits of proactive behavior, in other words.

Employee initiated (bottom row) requires the employee acting on relevant information. This means the employee is free to choose (or not choose) to behave proactively. With the right information, they're better placed to make these decisions. It's then up to the employee to determine what action to take, or whether to take any action, in other words.

In the context of this framework, shared purpose is facilitated by management to promote useful proactive behavior. By sharing their vision, the leader inspires their team to contribute to that aim. With a clear purpose, it's more apparent where the employee's independent judgment is needed.

With boundary management (the other manager-initiated strategy), it's the manager's role to identify where the boundaries are for independent judgment. Based on these parameters, the employee is free to choose to act independently or not. The confidence to act or not is largely dependent on how well their leader defined these boundaries.

Information exchange and proactive accountability are employee initiated. Like shared purpose, information exchange is designed to stimulate employee initiative in the right areas. Proactive accountability is a strategy that contains proactive behavior. As I said, the employee is made aware they can use their independent judgment, but they're ultimately responsible for its outcome. In both cases, the employee is the initiator.

## Other Considerations

There are some other issues worth noting in applying the framework. Inviting more employee enterprise is the first hurdle to overcome, except in the case of proactive accountability. When applied correctly by the leader, the three other strategies boost more employee empowerment.

Let's consider applying the framework in the context of the work people do, the organizational setting, and people's capabilities.

Proactive endeavors must support the nature of work being undertaken. The selection and use of strategies are dependent on the context. Solutions to problems and challenges vary and not all resolutions rely on independent judgment. Each of the four strategies is designed to overcome the proactive paradox in a different way. The leader should consider when to use each strategy.

One way to do this is to consider the dimensions of *task* and *people*. By "task," I refer to work activities. In a highly regulated government agency, for instance, confining employee initiative would be more important due to the standardization of most activities. Boundary management and proactive accountability are suited in these work settings, whereas the work of a startup business benefits more from invigorating employee enterprise, with the infinite growth and expansion opportunities of a virgin enterprise. Stimulating proactivity is the dominant consideration, with shared purpose and information exchange useful strategies.

Task also covers the functional operations within the organization. People working in "accounts" probably have less scope for showing initiative than in "sales and marketing," for instance. In these functional areas of the business, regulating and stimulating strategies would be used, respectively. The nature of the work and the type of tasks have a significant baring on the strategies deployed.

"People," in this context, refer to capabilities. In most cases, inexperienced employees need more guidance and direction than a bunch of seasoned and competent operators, for instance. Or, a new employee wouldn't be as capable of working autonomously, at least at the start of their career, as an experienced person. A skilled leader provides the newbie with clear boundaries. Semiskilled and unskilled workers may also rely on their manager for direction. Boundary management is an appropriate strategy in both cases.

Professionals and skilled workers require a different approach. With a strong skill set and proven track record, these employees have a better grasp of when to think for themselves, or at least, they may think they do! Shared purpose and information exchange are best used here. People, based on their experience and skills, will vary in what they need from their leader.

The know-how of a manager needs to be considered too. A novel manager, leading a team of experts, may have little choice than to rely on the team to use their judgment. For new managers leading a technically capable team, the two stimulating proactive strategies are suitable.

Conversely, a veteran manager with a good technical grasp, leading an inexperienced team, will need to be more hands-on. Restricting the team's scope for autonomous decision making is best. The two regulating proactivity strategies are better options.

The people and task dimension are a useful way to consider the application of the four strategies.

Table 6.2 is a summary of the four strategies, their application, and limitations.

*Table 6.2 Summary of the four strategies*

| Strategy | Definition | Application | Limitation |
|---|---|---|---|
| Shared purpose | Shared purpose aligns the needs and interests of the organization and individual. This alignment promises to stimulate enterprising behavior to achieve a clear purpose | The use of shared purpose is suitable when the leader wants to fully harness the enterprising qualities of employees to assist the organization to achieve its objectives | Given the complexities of organizational environments, aligning the needs and interests of the organization and employees are often difficult to accomplish |
| Boundary management | Boundary management involves careful communication of the kinds of initiative desired, and where it shouldn't be displayed | The use of boundary management is applicable in working environments that requires a mix of procedural and entrepreneurial work | Limiting enterprising qualities to specific situations may be frustrating to employees who like to work autonomously |
| Information exchange | Information exchange opens the communication channels between manager and employees to work collaboratively | Information exchange is useful for developing new strategies and direction that tap into employees' perspectives | This strategy requires high trust levels between managers and employees; such openness can make some managers feel vulnerable |
| Proactive accountability | Proactive accountability means letting employees know that they can exercise their independent judgment, but only at their own risk | The use of proactive accountability is appropriate in bureaucratic and regulatory organizations | This strategy holds few benefits for employees and limits independent judgment to exceptional circumstances |

The proactive framework does two things: lessens unwanted, unintended consequences of poor employee initiative and increases opportunities for constructive enterprise. Two solutions (boundary management and proactive accountability) do this by constraining employee initiative in unwanted areas. The other two (shared purpose and information exchange) mainly empower employees by aligning perspectives and improving communication.

---

# Where the Rubber Meets the Road

### Thinking Outside the Box

*Southwest's* senior vice president for corporate communication, Ginger Hardage, told participates at a conference a story about a Southwest pilot:

"On September 11, 2001, after terrorists had brought the planes down, all other planes that were already in the air were grounded. A Southwest plane was directed to land at an airport that Southwest did not serve, and the passengers and crew were put up in a hotel. When Southwest management called the hotel to enquire about the passengers and crew, they were told that no one was there—the pilot had taken everyone from that plane out to the movies."

"There's no manual from which to learn that," said Hardage. "At Southwest, employees are encouraged to make decisions from the heart, and in turn, these proactive gestures provide positive benefits to the customers and the company."

In a recent survey, 76 percent of Americans think that a company's treatment of its employees is a major factor in whether customers will purchase from that company. As Southwest makes its employees the top priority, Southwest is really making its customers come first, too (Baker 2009).[2]

---

Leaders can use a combination of strategies. For the leader dealing with complex and fluid work situations, it's imperative they constantly communicate the necessary outcomes to their team. The leader wanting to promote a shared purpose with their team may feel inclined to combine this strategy with information exchange. Information exchange supports individual and organizational objectives.

Alternatively, in more regulated work setting, the leader will probably favor a different combination of approaches. In these workplaces, narrowing the pathway for empowerment is more desirable. Where using independent judgment is less appealing, boundary management and proactive accountability can be used. Boundary management and proactive accountability are a natural pairing in regulating employee enterprise.

Other combinations of the four strategies are possible, but less likely. When unnatural combinations are applied, it would suit multifaceted project-based work. With major project work, where getting the balance between enterprise and bureaucratic considerations is paramount, a variety of strategies would be useful.

The mindset of the leader will also dictate their use of the four strategies. Conservative managers, for instance, will be drawn to boundary management and proactive accountability. Employees, eager to flex their independent judgment muscles, will challenge the traditional view of management authority. This will threaten some managers. However, most managers, regardless of their attitudes about leadership, appreciate the value of proactive employees. But some draw the line at being criticized, even when it is constructive. Managers, in my experience, are more defensive about upward feedback—even when it's well-intended—than they'll admit. Wanting employees to think independently, but not wanting constructive criticism, is like playing a contact sport and thinking one will never get injured!

Wanting team members to think independently while being closed to criticism sends a confusing signal. This muddling message reinforces the proactive paradox. For instance, if the manager gets defensive when receiving constructive criticism, the employee may—for self-preservation—go into their shell. Leaders need to be open to upward feedback and even encourage it.

Another major stumbling block is the manager who sees themselves as the *boss*. This attitude conveys an impression to those they lead that the manager has all the answers, or at least they think they do. They aren't receptive to being questioned or challenged. Even when the employee thinks their manager is wrong—which they'll be from time-to-time—they know that verbalizing this may be career limiting. So, why risk it? A transformational leader—viewing employees as partners—is will be open to feedback, on the other hand. Being willing to receive—and even invite—negative feedback is a starting point for a leader wanting empowered team members.

If people know from first-hand experience that their manager is sensitive to any criticism, they'll retreat. They understandably (and regrettably) fall back to complying with the conventional demarcation of responsibilities. The manager is left to be directive and the employee merely carrying out their instructions. It's the manager—not just the employee—who needs to change their thinking about their role for the proactive paradox to be settled. We covered this mindset change in Chapter 3.

Follow the manager's direction without question is considered a sign of loyalty in the traditional relationship. But if loyalty is blindly following the boss's instructions, then upward feedback will not occur. When the leader's judgment is faulty, or their ethics suspect, feedback is imperative for course correction. What's more, constructive criticism should extend beyond standards and ethics.

Aside from upward feedback, under the old contract, if something isn't openly permitted by the manager, it's prohibited. But nowadays, with relentless change and uncertainty, people need to think for themselves and not wait for the manager's consent. So, the opposite needs to apply; that is, whatever isn't expressly prohibited is permissible. What's more, even when the leader gives an instruction, a forward-thinking employee should hesitate occasionally to form their own judgment. Taking this responsibility can sometimes lead to a more informed decision.

Expecting people to use independent judgment means employees are sharing the leadership role. This new contract raises an interesting question: *If the employee role is evolving closer to the managerial role, what then becomes of the managerial role?* With the rise of employee empowerment, it assumes that the formal leadership role is less relevant. It's not. Although the leadership role I'm describing is vastly different from the old them and us relationship, it's just as relevant. If anything, it's even more germane. The kind of leadership I'm advocating is the catalyst for fostering the appropriate environment for employees' enterprise to flourish.

In a VUCA world, employee initiative—when channeled correctly—is fundamental to organizational success. Good leadership involves establishing and communicating a clear overarching vision and letting people know how they can contribute to achieving the outcome. The transformational leader therefore facilitates team members to exercise their enterprising qualities in specified areas.

But we need a dose of reality. We need to acknowledge these new roles won't automatically remove the roadblocks for empowerment to thrive. A leader and team member embracing the new contract will still be conflicted from time-to-time about their roles. Team members still need guidance and information to use their independent judgment. The four strategies we are discussing here are intended to lessen the disparities. This framework helps team members understand where they can and cannot adopt their independent judgment. Without some clarity, two problems will inevitably occur: Either proactive behavior will be too dysfunctional, or it will be too infrequent.

The collaborative relationship I illustrated in Chapter 2 signals changes in the way leaders and team members interact. A team member should feel comfortable respectfully questioning the leader's decision making, where in past they may have said nothing, for instance. Leaders should be receptive to constructive criticism from team members, where in the past they may have shunned it. These types of conversations aren't always comfortable. But without authentic communication, based on greater parity in the employment relationship, the proactive paradox will prevail.

The proactive employee is an asset to a business. But a proactive employee isn't a commodity to be purchased via a recruitment and selection process. Although some people are naturally more proactive than others, empowerment is a by-product of the employment relationship, it's not a commodity or technique. While independent judgment varies in employees, people are capable and willing to think for themselves. The working relationship will either encourage or discourage autonomy.

There's a personal price to pay for people to hold out a fixed mindset about the traditional employment relationship. The manager stubbornly resists the momentum toward the new contract, will ultimately be redundant or replaced. Employees choosing to be passive recipients of their boss's directive, limit their career options and will be replaced eventually too. Replacing people is costly and an unpleasant experience. Even so, the costs of harboring people with a traditional mindset are becoming increasingly outweighed by the necessity to move them on.

In summary, the proactive framework arouses desirable employee enterprise and limits it to where it's best served. The common theme supporting the four strategies is better dialog between leader and team member. The framework improves and refines information flow. This inevitably boosts performance. Everyone benefits. Team members who have more autonomy and control are more engaged. And managers who expedite an empowered team are more trusted and more influential.

In the next chapter, we consider some specific ways leaders can apply the strategy of shared purpose.

# Top 10 Points

1. The role of the leader applying boundary management is to identify and communicate appropriate and inappropriate conditions for exercising the independent judgment.
2. The proactive framework has two dimensions: Stimulating or regulating proactivity and manager or employee initiated.
3. Stimulate proactivity emphasizes encouraging over constraining proactive behavior.
4. Regulating proactivity focuses more on discouraging unsuitable proactive behavior over inspiring it.
5. Manager initiated entails the leader providing guidance to team member.
6. Employee initiated refers to employees acting based on relevant information.
7. Shared purpose is facilitated by management to promote useful proactive behavior.
8. With boundary management, it's the manager's role to identify where the boundaries are for independent judgment.
9. Like shared purpose, information exchange is designed to stimulate employee initiative in the right areas.
10. Proactive accountability is a strategy that contains proactive behavior.

# CHAPTER 7

# Shared Purpose Practices

If the leader actions vary from their words, it's
futile expecting integrity from others.

*On April 14, 1970, when an oxygen tank on Apollo 13 exploded
during the third crewed mission to the Moon, it appeared that
the three-member crew was doomed. Hearing the dreaded words,
"Houston, we've had a problem," NASA knew that it had to abort
the mission and find a way of bringing the three astronauts back
200,000 miles to Earth immediately. Individuals, teams, and groups
came together, poured over data, ideated on blackboards, restrooms,
and over water coolers, to come up with solutions to address a serious
problem, tried to implement them, failed—and tried again until they
succeeded. For two days, the goal of saving the three astronauts' lives
became everyone's purpose (Nayer 2014).[1]*

The aim of applying the shared purpose strategy is to align the needs
of the leader and their team members. The more agreement, the more
chance the teams' behavior will accord with their leader's vision. Using
this strategy means making sure that everyone is on the same page. A
clear purpose gives people sufficient confidence to apply their independent judgment to accomplish the goal.

In this chapter, we consider four practices to promote a shared
purpose. They are as follows:

- Modeling the way
- Developing a team values charter
- Offering support and encouragement
- Providing regular feedback

These practices foster the conditions for team members to be proactive.

# Modeling the Way

*Modeling the way* is one of five leadership practices popularized by Jim Kouzes and Barry Posner in their book, The Five Practices of Exemplary Leadership (Kouzes and Posner 2011).[2] The practices are model the way, inspire a shared vision, challenge the process, enable others to act, and encourage the heart. By modeling the way, the leader's actions are setting an example for team members to follow. In short, the leader is leading by example. Though all five practices are relevant for a leader to practice, I'll focus on modeling the way and how it's relevant to cultivating a shared purpose.

What a leader says—but, more importantly, what they do—sets the standard for others to follow. In times of change and uncertainty—which is most of the time—a leader's example paves the way forward. Chaos reigns in times of transformation. People can easily lose sight of the bigger picture. Leaders signal their priorities by the actions they take. People notice. A strong leader removes barriers, overcomes obstacles, and minimizes red tape in times of turmoil. The transformational leader, staying true to their purpose, shows others what needs to be done. Through their modeling, people know what's expected of them and how they can contribute.

Modeling the way opens the door for others to be resourceful. Observing their leader when their words and actions match, followers are clear when independent should and shouldn't be used. The leader signposts the road ahead by their actions, in other words, giving people faith to act according to that direction.

Furthermore, the exemplary leaders breathe life into their vision with positivity and optimism. They inspire followers to embrace that purpose. This modeling includes remaining calm when things go wrong and making sure their actions are in sync with the team's values. As Kouzes and Posner reminds us,

> values influence every aspect of our lives: our moral judgments, our responses to others, our commitments to personal and organizational goals (Kouzes and Posner 2011).[3]

Leaders choose to go first, demonstrating a can-do attitude with as much humor and optimism they can muster. Their actions persuade others to buy-in to their purpose. Most managers can *talk the talk*, but *walking the walk* is what gets noticed. People follow actions, not words. Kouzes and Posner point out that,

> When people see you doing what you say, then they have the evidence that you mean it. Otherwise, it's just words. Your actions send the loudest signals about what other people should be doing (Kouzes and Posner 2011).[4]

If the leader actions vary from their words, it's futile expecting integrity from others.

Most typically underrate the significance of modeling the actions they want others to follow. But exceptional leaders model the way they want their team members to feel, think, and act. For instance, when a leader owns their mistakes and fixes them, the team will do the same. By admitting fault, the leader reduces the fear of failure in others. Being afraid of failure is the reason people play it safe and don't act proactively, even when it's called for.

The proactive paradox's main stumbling block is incongruence between the leader's rhetoric and their actions. Saying you want people to back their own judgment while indulging in micromanagement is confusing (and irritating), for example. The practice of modeling the way is fundamental to effective leadership and sets the platform for developing a shared purpose.

---

## Where the Rubber Meets the Road

### Leaders are the Best Learners

Good leaders spend time thinking about other leaders they've observed and the characteristics they admire. They then try to adopt these traits in their own repertoire. Effective leaders ask themselves: *How can I emulate these traits in my leadership style?* Leadership isn't about trying to be someone else; rather, it is about embracing these characteristics as part of their own style and approach. This requires heightened self-awareness and personal insight about the leader's strengths and opportunities for growth. They then apply these attributes in their daily actions and communications. As Kouzes and Posner put it, the best leaders are the best learners.

# Develop a Team Values Charter

Adhering to values in a team builds trust and cohesion. And heightened trust opens communication channels and cooperation. When trust is present, people support one another; they don't want to let each other down. Furthermore, people feel obligated to develop their capabilities and give their best. When people trust those they work closely with, they become a team and feel a sense of mutual obligation.

Creating a team values charter is a great trust building practice. I explained this in my book (coauthored with Aubrey Warren), *Conversations at Work: Promoting a Culture of Conversation in the Changing Workplace* (Baker and Warren 2015).[5]

Briefly, here's how it works.

Ask your team members to respond to the following five questions:

1. What one value is most important to you when working in a team?
2. How do you define your value?
3. Why is this value important to you?
4. What type of behaviors violate this value?
5. What type of behaviors are consistent with this value?

To illustrate, here's my response to the five questions:

1. What one value is most important to you when working in a team?
   (a) *Respect.*
2. How do you define your value?
   (a) *Respect to me means being prepared to listen to another point-of-view from a team member in an open and nonjudgmental way, even if you don't necessarily agree with their perspective.*
3. Why is this value important to you?
   (a) *This value of respect is important to me because I believe we ought to be encouraging diversity in the way we think and operate as a team. And if we are prepared to respect the views of others that we don't necessarily agree with, it will encourage others to speak up.*

4. What type of behaviors violate this value?
   (a) *I think someone interrupting another colleague before he or she has finished fully expressing their point-of-view is inappropriate. In my mind, this is disrespectful.*
5. What type of behaviors are consistent with this value?
   (a) *Actively listening to a different point-of-view with respect and interest.*

After everyone has completed their written responses, invite each person to share their replies to the five questions with the rest of the team. Consistent with modeling the way, the leader starts with their answers. You are setting the right example by starting. Invite others to ask questions as each person articulates their answers. This exercise should be interactive and not a series of individual presentations. The more dialog and informality in the room, the better.

Once everyone has shared their responses, you have the contents for the charter. With a team of six, including the leader, for instance, you have six values—assuming each person had a different value. So, the charter will contain six values.

The statement defining each value comes from the originator's response to the second question: *How do you define your value?* To illustrate, consider my value: *Respect*. Respect can mean many different things. It can mean anything from showing basic courteous to treating people as equals. In my illustration, respect is *being prepared to listen to another point-of-view from a team member in an open and nonjudgmental way, even if you don't necessarily agree with their perspective*. This is captured in the charter.

If several people have identified the same value, these team members collaborate to develop a statement they are happy with. For example, if one person defines *respect* as *listening to others* and another defines *respect* as *treating people courteously*, a combined statement might be: *To listen and be courteous to colleagues*. The key point is that everyone's perspective is included in the charter.

When the wording of the defining statement is clear and reflects the sentiments of the contributing team member(s), the team values charter is done. It can be framed and put on the wall of the regular meeting room. The charter can also be distributed and displayed prominently on the desktops of the six team members, reminding them of their collective agreement.

Although straightforward, don't be fooled by its simplicity—it's enormously potent. Team members have an emotionally connection to their charter via a value they strongly believe in. Put simply: the team *own* the charter.

It's then up to the team leader to use the charter to guide and inform the actions of the team. The leader can use the charter to provide feedback and develop shared purpose around a set of values.

Trust is an essential ingredient of an effective and well-functioning team. Trust is like the mortar that holds a brick wall together. It contributes to psychological safety—one of foundational human requirements psychologist Abraham Maslow identifies in his *Hierarchy of Needs*.[6] When people feel secure in the company of others, they also feel more comfortable to open up, take suitable risks, and expose their vulnerabilities.

Distrust in teams, on the other hand, leads to counterproductive behavior. Some of the obvious symptoms of low trust are as follows:

- Following the procedures manual, when initiative is expected
- Minimal fresh thinking and no new ideas
- Limited cooperation and no collaboration
- Reduced performance

People operating in a zero-trust environment spend their energy protecting themselves and their interests—time that should be better directed to accomplishing the team's purpose.

Trust is the fuel that drives knowledge sharing. Several studies show a link between trust and knowledge attainment (Hsiao-Wen Ho, Ghauri, and Larimo 2018).[7] If team members trust one another, they're more likely to share their knowledge and communicate more frequently and openly. The team values charter is a practice that builds trust.

## Offering Support and Encouragement

Former U.S. president, Theodore Roosevelt, is attributed as saying,

No one cares how much you know, until they know how much you care (Goodreads).[8]

This reminds us that all the persuasive techniques available will fail if the leader neglects the *care factor*. People need to feel they're supported. If they are backed, people usually are comfortable using their own judgment.

What's more, genuine encouragement and ample support bring out the best in others. Expressing appreciation, acknowledge contributions, and celebrate achievements are illustrations of encouragement and support. Recognition is a powerful motivation that feeding our need for worth. "Followers want to feel significant," says Robert Goffee and Gareth Jones in their article, "Why Should Anyone Be Led by You?" (Goffee and Jones 2000).[9] People yearn for acknowledgment.

Yet, it's remarkable that even though we crave some recognition, leaders give it sparingly, if at all. Maybe old school managers think that they need to be "hard," and recognition is too "soft." Whatever the misconception, leaders who affirm, recognize, and appreciate colleagues strengthen unity and purpose.

One of the simplest and most effective—yet most neglected forms of encouragement—can be expressed in two words: *thank you. Thank you for using your initiative. Thank you for staying back late to complete that project. Thank you for speaking up at this morning's meeting and expressing your point-of-view. Thank you for dealing with that customer so professionally under difficult circumstances.* Thanking people for their discretionary contributions promotes more independent judgment.

Here's a suggestion. Tomorrow, commit to having three brief conversations that are encouraging and supportive. If nothing else, it forces you to look for things that merit praise. Managers spot errors and feel obliged to point out these occurrences to the offender. That's okay; it's your job to fix mistakes. But try balancing constructive criticism with praise and encouragement if you aren't already doing this. If you do more of this, with the same conviction as picking up errors, you'll be pleasantly surprised, if you're not use to doing this. It'll positively affect morale, engagement, motivation, and general goodwill.

Being supportive and encouraging instills confidence in people to back themselves when the opportunity arises.

## Providing Regular Feedback

Feedback provides people with a sense of certainty. Recipients of feedback know whether they're on- or off-track. Feedback can be positive or constructive, or a combination of both. It can come from several sources, including the manager, colleagues, stakeholders, or themselves. Regardless of its source, the intent of feedback is to either reinforce that the person is on-purpose, or not.

A good way to structure your feedback is to use the SBI model (Center of Creative Leadership).[10] SBI stands for:

1. Situation
2. Behavior
3. Impact

When you structured constructive feedback using SBI, the receiver is less likely to take it personally. They understand the context (situation), the specific actions (behavior) that need correcting, and its consequences (impact). By following this format, the leader avoids the common trap of vague generalizations that are unhelpful to the recipient.

*Situation* refers to the critical incident prompting the need for feedback. Referring to a specific event, the feedback is contextualized, giving the person a reference point, or setting to consider. For example, you might start with: "During this morning's meeting … " The next step is to describe the specific behavior you want to draw attention to.

*Behavior* describes the action (or inaction) you want to give feedback on. Referring to the previous illustration, I might then say, "when you interrupted Justin twice … " The behavior should be specific. Mention the behavior, but don't judge. Words like, *shouldn't*, *don't*, and *can't*, aren't necessary and will probably prompt a defensive response from the recipient.

*Impact* explains the implications of the behavior. Following the illustration, I might then say, "you may have discouraged Justin from contributing their ideas in future." In this case, the receiver may try to defend themselves by replying that they were merely "correcting" him. It's okay to empathize here. You can reply alone the lines of "while you're probably right, my concern is that you may hinder Justin from offering suggestions in future meetings." It's simple and effective.

So, in summary, the feedback for this example, using SBI, is:

During this morning's meeting (situation), when you interrupted Justin twice (behavior), you may have discouraged him from contributing their ideas in future (impact).

Regular feedback ensures that the work people do is consistent with the team's purpose. Feedback lets people know how they are tracking, in other words. With frequent feedback, using the SBI model, people are clearer about the role they should be playing. Feedback instills confidence. Team members gain a better understanding of when they should (and shouldn't) use their independent judgment and how this contributes to the team's purpose.

The practices of modeling the way, developing a set of clear values to govern behavior, providing support and encouragement, and giving consistent feedback all align people's contribution to a common purpose. This builds belief and mutual understanding.

In the next chapter, we look at practices supporting boundary management.

## Top 10 Points

1. The aim of applying the shared purpose strategy is to align the needs of the leader and their team members.
2. What a leader says—but, more importantly, what they do—sets the standard for others to follow.
3. Observing their leader when their words and actions match, followers are clear when independent judgment should and shouldn't be used.
4. Creating a team values charter is a great trust building practice.
5. When people feel secure in the company of others, they also feel more comfortable to open up, take suitable risks, and expose their vulnerabilities.

6. Genuine encouragement and ample support bring out the best in others.
7. Being supportive and encouraging instills confidence in people to back themselves when the opportunity arises.
8. Feedback provides people with a sense of certainty.
9. A good way to structure feedback is to use the SBI model.
10. The practices of modeling the way, developing a set of clear values to govern behavior, providing support and encouragement, and giving consistent feedback all align people's contribution to a common purpose.

# CHAPTER 8

# Boundary Management Practices

Instead of answering questions, the leader's role is to ask questions.

*Denise brainstorms with her team on when it's suitable to show independent judgment and when it's not. She draws three columns on the whiteboard. In the left-hand column Denise asks her team to identify examples of when the team should follow set processes and procedures. She lists these instances. Denise then asks her team to identify circumstances when it's suitable to use their own judgment. She records these cases in the right-hand column. And then Denise invites her colleagues to identify situations were either may be applicable; that is, where one can follow a set process or think originally, and she lists these in the middle column. By doing this simple exercise, Denise clarifies the boundaries for independent judgment with her team's assistance.*

Boundary management has a dual purpose. On one hand, this strategy identifies the circumstances where initiative is desirable. And on the other hand, it pinpoints where initiative is not welcome. In short, this strategy defines the boundaries for employee enterprise. Boundary management assumes that the more certain someone is about these boundaries, the more confident they feel in performing their duties. This strategy is designed to confine independent judgment to specific instances and circumstances.

Two practices help to manage these boundaries:

- Facilitating a team debriefing
- Coaching team members.

These two practices clarify the extents and limits of proactive behavior.

# Facilitating a Team Debriefing

When a significant event occurs at work, it offers a golden opportunity to learn. Debriefing after a workplace episode—whether a positive or negative experience—is useful to consider how similar future situations can be managed better. How can a similar situation be approached in future? Next time is independent judgment appropriate or should we follow standard practices? are questions that should be considered. One of the best debrief methods for boundary management is the After-Action Review (AAR).

According to management guru Peter Senge in *The Dance of Change*:

> The Army's After-action Review (AAR) is arguably one of the most successful organizational learning methods yet devised. Yet, most every corporate effort to graft these truly innovative practices into their culture has failed because, again and again, people reduce the living practice of AAR's to a sterile technique (Senge 1999).[1]

High praise indeed.

What is an AAR?

The AAR is a debriefing practice that is designed to share lessons learned from the past to make improvements for the future. An AAR can be done during or at the completion of any project. The AAR is versatile and can be applied to improve decision making. An AAR can be done casually in the corridor or more formally in the meeting room. The method is designed to constructively consider an incident or project while it is fresh in the minds of those involved.

The spirit of the AAR is based on openness and learning—it's not a tool for apportioning blame or finding fault. In team conversations, lessons learned are shared and documented for future reference if necessary.

AARs were originally developed—and still extensively used—by the U.S. army. The business world has been slow to appreciate its value and apply it. And unfortunately, many organizations that have adopted the AAR use it as a quality check, rather than a tool for improvement. Using the AAR as a box ticking exercise, rather than a tool of continuous improvement, diminish its usefulness.

The AAR is effective in a wide range of situations. At one end of the spectrum, AARs can be done by one or two people as a five-minute debriefing conversation on the spur of the moment. Or, at the other end of the spectrum, it can be used to structure a day-long off-site meeting between several stakeholders involved in a large-scale project. Activities suitable for an AAR require three features, however. These characteristics are a fixed beginning and endpoint, an identifiable purpose, and a desire to improve decision making for the future.

There are several versions of the AAR. But I think the form most suitable for managing the boundaries for proactive behavior is based on three key questions:

- What was done well?
- What could have been improved?
- What improvements can be made for the future?

These three questions focus the mind of participants on appraising the positive and negative aspects of the project or incident.

Apart from gleaning the gems of wisdom from the shared experiences of contributors, the collaborative process fosters a sense of commitment to the agreed outcomes of the review. This commitment is generated from positive participation from everyone and a group consensus. Team members, clearer about how decision making needs to change in future, experience a sense of obligation to apply the key learnings.

Here are some ideas for applying an AAR:

- When a new set of procedures or way of working has been introduced and used for the first time
- After a busy period where capacity was stretched
- Following a trial period of a new system or procedure
- After a major training activity
- Between two work shifts

This list isn't conclusive. These examples do, however, provide you with a useful starting point.

The AAR is a helpful tool for managing the extents and limits of proactive behavior. Insights about where initiative was valuable can be gained from the debrief. Simultaneously, an understanding of where following process is more beneficial than using independent judgment can be discussed and agreed upon. With everyone participating in these review discussions, individuals feel a sense of heightened obligation to apply the lessons learned.

AARs are also useful for sharing tacit knowledge during the life of a project, incident, or activity. It provides a gateway for seasoned team members to communicate their experience. Legitimate shortcuts that are second nature to experienced colleagues can be conveyed for the benefit of the whole team, for instance. Key learning points can be summarized by the leader, while it is fresh in people's minds.

Despite its name ("after action"), the review does not have to be performed at the end of a project or activity. An AAR can be performed after each identifiable milestone of a project or major activity. Doing a review at discernible phases means it becomes a method for continuous learning. Lessons learned can be applied in the next phase of the project.

Individual can also use an AAR for personal reflection. For instance, you can take a few minutes to reflect on something you did yesterday, such as attending a meeting with an important stakeholder, dealing with a complaint, or making an important telephone call. What do my reflections tell me about altering my approach next time? Where is it useful to back my own judgment? When is being risk adverse necessary by following the system? are useful questions to consider.

## Coaching Team Members

Apart from using the AAR practice, one-on-one coaching is also helpful for clarifying boundaries and responsibilities. One of the best known and most effective coaching models is GROW. While no one person can be identified as the originator of *GROW*, Graham Alexander, Alan Fine, and Sir John Whitmore all made significant contributions toward developing the model.[2]

GROW stands for

- Goal
- Reality

- Options
- What next?

Let's explore these four steps.

*Goal:* The intention in the first stage of GROW is to set a goal or desired outcome. A clear goal means the coachee walks away from the coaching conversation with a tangible objective if they don't already have one. And as leader, you are also clear what the other person wants to achieve.

When someone comes to you with an issue, problem, or challenge and wants to *dump* on you, politely stop them and ask: What is the ideal outcome you are trying to achieve? This question forces the other person to articulate what success looks like. If the other person can't articulate the ideal outcome, it means they haven't thought it through.

Furthermore, if the coachee doesn't know where they are headed, then it's impossible for them to know where to start. It's therefore important to ask the person to consider the result they're aiming for. Your coaching sessions should start by identifying the goal. But it's possible that the coachee may not be able to articulate a specific goal at the outset, as I said. Persevere. Asking questions and probe. Guide the other person to identify the ideal state.

Here are some questions that might help to clarify the goal:

- For you to be satisfied, what would the outcome be?
- What are you trying to achieve?
- How will you know you have been successful?
- What are you aiming for?

*Reality:* Once the coachee has articulated a desired outcome, you can then pivot to a different set of questions: What's getting in the way? or What's stopping you getting to this result? These questions guide the coachee to recognize the barriers that may be preventing them achieving the goal. Identifying the roadblocks after determining an objective means *only* considering those things that are the main barriers in the way. Peripheral matters needn't be discussed.

Too much time is often consumed discussing irrelevant or minor conditions blocking the path to a solution. These extraneous matters are often raised and discussed and aren't helpful; they produce a downward spiral of negativity. This wastes valuable time.

Leadership development programs teach us the value of listening. But listening and not interrupting someone when they are having a whinge is usually counterproductive. People understandably want to get things off their chest from time-to-time. But instead of passively listening on these occasions, a better approach is to steer the conversation to the main barriers. Discussing circumstances outside our control are energy sapping and pointless. What are the core factors preventing success? should be the focus.

At this stage in the coaching session, by asking and discussing one or two questions, you have assisted the coachee to clarify the ideal outcome and recognize the main obstacle in its attainment.

When the main barriers have been identified, the solutions are more likely to be relevant. Your job as coach during the reality stage is to help the coachee identify the main barriers to a successful outcome. Asking good questions is like peeling away the layers of an onion and getting to the core of the problem.

Try these questions to grasp the reality:

- What are the key factors getting in the way of you achieving this goal?
- What are the main barriers to success?
- What's stopping you achieve this outcome?
- Can you identify the main obstacle?

*Options:* Once the coachee can pinpoint the major hurdles, your role now is to help them to generate some options to achieve the desired outcome. This will probably be the most challenging part for you as coach.

Ask the coachee what their options are for a successful outcome. The options stage of the coaching session is tricky because you probably know what their options are. It's tempting to therefore offer these choices, based on your experience. The answers are likely to be on the tip of your tongue. Bit your tongue until it bleeds!

Volunteering your solution—no matter how well intended and work-able it is—isn't helpful. Why? You want the other person to *own* the solution, to be emotionally committed to resolving their problem. Giving the coachee the answer is not the answer. By offering your wisdom, you are reinforcing the proactive paradox. Your team member will become more dependent on you for answers, and so there is no need for them to think for themselves.

Furthermore, the model includes the word *options*, not *option*. Options imply that there is more than one possibility. By asking for several options—instead of one—you open the prospect of finding numerous solutions. On hearing one option, ask them what other options they could consider. Be patient and wait for the coachee to offer other alternatives. Don't judge. Don't evaluate. Just listen and ask for more options.

Let's recap. At this stage, you both know what the ideal outcome is (goal), what's stopping the coachee from achieve that outcome (reality) and discussed several options for resolving the issue (options). Good progress so far.

---

## Where the Rubber Meets the Road

### The Process of Self-Discovery

In most of my coaching conversations, when I use GROW, I've been astonished at the inherent capability of people to see their way through issues, resolve problems, and identify development needs. Provided I don't answer my own questions, the other person is invited to think for themselves; they are applying their independent judgment. In most cases, it's not necessary for me to intrude overtly in a natural process of self-discovery.

---

In the Options phase—like the other phases of GROW—the best strategy is to ask open-ended questions. Successful coaching conversations don't always need to draw out particularly novel ideas. Oftentimes, they bring previous thoughts into sharper focus and help the coachee decide whether certain choices are doable.

Before asking them to consider their options, it's possible that the coachee will ask for your advice. It's natural for them to be interested in their leader's opinion. What's more, the employee may think it's the manager's job to give them the answers, particularly if they hold a conventional view of employment relationship. With a traditional mindset, they'll probably not believe it as their place to think for themselves. This isn't a license to you to start giving them advice, however, as tempting as it surely is. GROW is a practice that encourages initiative.

Nonetheless, the coachee, regardless of their view about the employment relationship, may be stumped for answers and need their manager's assistance. Or they may suggest an unrealistic or unsafe solution. What then does the coach do?

On these occasions, it's not the coach's job to *rescue* the coachee. The team member's responsibility is to do the heavy lifting. GROW is structured to enable the coachee to find a way forward that is viable. The coachee should have the freedom and autonomy to make their own choices and decisions. By asking questions, seeking clarification, and playing devil's advocate, the coach is helping the coachee to explore possibilities. So, be patient and help your team member to think about the problem more deeply.

In time, the coachee will in most cases arrive at several workable options to bridge the gap between where they want to go (goal) and where they are (reality). With patience and persistence, solutions will come. The coach may add some possible additional options, but only after the coachee has hit the wall, not before.

Here are some questions to generate options:

- What have you thought about doing to resolve this?
- What are your options?
- Who can I help you resolve this?
- What are some other possibilities?

*What next?* The "W" in GROW stands for *What next?* In this final stage, ask the coachee to consider their options and select the best way forward. Reassure the coachee that you will support them to act. Support may be simply affirming that they are on the right track (assuming they are) or taking an interest in their progress.

By now, the coachee should have several options to consider. The aim at this stage is to narrow the possibilities down into a workable plan, arriving at a final course-of-action, broken down into specific steps. As their coach, gently challenge them to follow through. Is it practical? What are the possible obstacles to the action steps? And what support will be required from you and others? are useful questions to ask.

This is where the rubber meets the road. *What next?* is the time to drill down to the details. This involves tangible actions, when they will be taken, who needs to be consulted, and how success will be evaluated. Whether the coaching session has been effective will depend on a well-defined and feasible plan.

If it's not apparent, ask the coachee why they chose the solution. Talking over their rationale for taking a certain course-of-action can build confidence in their line-of-thinking. Understanding the coachee's motives also gauges their conviction in their choice into action.

Here are some questions to guide *what next?* phase:

- Which of these options is the most feasible?
- Why have you chosen this course-of-action?
- What's the next step?
- What support will you need from me and others?

GROW offers a simple, practical, and comprehensive framework for leaders to facilitate productive coaching conversations. It's a great method for fostering engagement. Using GROW doesn't require unattainable skill, training in psychology, or a background in psychotherapy.

Two assumptions support GROW. Good coaching is about asking good questions. Secondly, it assumes that the person being coached is fully capable and willing to act. GROW assumes that the team member can take responsibility to be proactive, in other words. These assumptions are also relevant to boundary management.

It's a common misconception that coaching is about a leader imparting their knowledge, wisdom, and experience on the apprentice. I think managers—when faced with an employee wanting answers—tend to spoon-feed them with answers for two reasons. First, the manager—being human—craves the feeling of being needed. By being the source of *vital* information, the manager feels valued and appreciated. It's like a quick sugar hit. But managers need to remind themselves that they're not in the business of solving people's problems. Instead of answering questions, the leader's role is to ask questions. To paraphrase that familiar proverb,

> give a man a fish and you feed him for a day; teach a man to fish and you feed him for a lifetime.[3]

Using GROW is all about *enabling* the other person to achieve sustainable success.

The second reason the manager finds it seductive to answer a team member's question is simply that it's quick. Thinking that it will take too much unnecessary time to do otherwise, the manager offers their solution. Why not just give them the answer and move on? is the common belief. But the reality is opposite; it ultimately takes more time giving people a solution. How so? By giving an employee the answer, the manager is training them to be dependent. It encourages employees to come back again for more answers rather than think for themselves. That's time consuming.

Furthermore, giving people a quick response creates the impression that the manager has *all* the answers. The employee will perpetually go to them for answers on a wide range of matters, particularly when they notice the manager is happy to respond. It's convenient for the employee—much more convenient than stretching their brain by thinking for themselves. This conditions employees to be reliant on the boss, not self-reliant (learning to catch the fish). And as I said, the manager rationalizes that responding with a quick answer saves time. But in their haste to impart their wisdom and experience, the manager fails to realize that it trains people to incessantly interrupt them on trivial matters.

The know-it-all manager may consider using GROW as time wasting. But listening to team member long-winded explanation about a problem they have is more time consuming. The GROW format reduces—not increases—time by conditioning team members to be self-sufficient.

And being self-reliant means the leader gets fewer frivolous interruptions. Using GROW saves you time.

Another advantage of GROW is its adaptability. GROW is suitable for resolving most workplace problems. It trains people to think for themselves. It establishes boundaries and consistent with developing the collaborative employment relationship we discussed in Chapter 3.

Managers are functional, structured, and goal driven. GROW ticks all these boxes. The coaching process facilitates tangible outcomes and is, therefore, functional. GROW's four steps provide an easy to remember structure. And its focus is on outcomes which suits the goal-driven manager. GROW is easy to remember, is easy to administer, and gets results.

Apart from impromptu meetings, GROW works for prearranged coaching session too. The structure and process remain the same. It is a collaborative process regardless of how it is used. GROW is useful in all coaching contexts.

Although easy to use and adaptable, GROW does require a shift in thinking. It means moving from *telling* to *asking*. Its effectiveness comes from enabling the coachee to be self-reliant. The coach's role is to support the coachee to find their own answer to the dilemma, problem, or challenge they face. GROW is contrary to the superior dictating a solution to a subordinate—the basis of the them and us employment relationship we discussed in Chapter 2. If telling is all that's required, the manager may as well send an e-mail with specific instructions to the employee!

Growth and development come from taking ownership and responsibility for a person's actions and results. By asking thought-provoking questions, the leader is challenging the coachee to do the necessary thinking to solve their problems. The coachee is expected to collaborate and engage in the GROW format. This challenges the employee to adjust their thinking too.

Finally, GROW is a tool to prompt independent judgment when needed and understand when following protocol is a better option—it is a practice well suited for boundary management.

In the next chapter, we look at information exchange practices that work.

# Top 10 Points

1. Boundary management has a dual purpose. On one hand, this strategy identifies the circumstances where initiative is desirable. And on the other hand, it pinpoints where initiative is not welcome.

2. The AAR is a debriefing practice that is designed to share lessons learned from the past to make improvements for the future.

3. The spirit of the AAR is based on openness and learning—it's not a tool for apportioning blame or finding fault.

4. The AAR is effective in a wide range of situations.

5. The three key questions for facilitating an AAR are: What was done well? What could have been improved? What improvements can be made in the future?

6. One of the best known and most effective coaching models is GROW.

7. GROW stands for Goal, Reality, Options, and What next?

8. Two assumptions support GROW. Good coaching is about asking good questions. Secondly, it assumes that the person being coached is fully capable and willing to act.

9. GROW is suitable for resolving most workplace problems.

10. GROW is a tool to prompt independent judgment when needed and understand when following protocol is a better option—it is a practice well suited for boundary management.

# CHAPTER 9

# Information Exchange Practices

If (a team purpose statement) is constructed by the leader—which is often the case—they will undoubtedly be sold on the statement. But … no-one else will probably be as excited and enthusiastic about it, no matter how great it is.

*I recall being asked to work with a local government authority in Australia several years ago. The organization wanted me to work with the newly elected Council to develop a brand-new purpose statement they were all committed to. This was a daunting task since each of the eight Councilors were elected on different and often conflicting platforms. Each Councilor, elected by their community, was expected to honor their policy stances in the new Council.*

*How can I gain agreement on a purpose for all members of Council?*

*I decided to ask each Councilor to write a statement that best reflected their purpose. After doing so, I asked each Councilor to pair up with another colleague and merge their two statements into one, reflecting the sentiments of both representatives. Then, I asked the pairs to join with another pair and go through the same process. Finally, we ended up with two statements and merged them to come up with one overarching purpose. All of this took 40 minutes! And all Councilors were committed to their purpose statement.*

Information exchange is a strategy that aims to open the communication channels between a manager and employee. By swapping information and perspectives between the leader and team member, both have the potential to be on the same page. This strategy is compatible with the collaborative employment relationship model I illustrated in Chapter 3.

Information exchange essentially shares the leadership responsibility among the team. Aligning perspectives fosters independent judgment in pursuit of a common purpose.

The strategy enables a common understanding and clear direction. Information exchange builds trust between the leader and their team. Such openness may make some managers feel vulnerable. But the benefits of sharing perspectives outweigh the insecurities traditional managers may have.

Two information exchange practices we cover in this chapter are as follows:

- Creating a team purpose statement
- Creating a behavior agreement

These two practices are also helpful to promote a shared purpose.

## Creating a Team Purpose Statement

This exercise has been adapted from *Hyper Island*.[1] I cover this activity in my previous book, *Winning Teams: The Eight Characteristics of High Performing Teams* (Baker 2021),[2] in more detail. It's been modified, based on my experience in assisting many teams to develop their own purpose statement.

The two practices work in tandem. Both exercises take little time to do and inspire constructive proactive behavior. The purpose statement clarifies a team's direction, and the behavior agreement identified the actions necessary for the purpose to be achieved. These exercises address two key fundamental questions: *Why do we exist?* and *How should we behave to achieve our purpose?* Defining a clear purpose and the necessary behaviors emboldens initiative by improving the line of sight between work and the team's direction.

The outcome of the exercises is a one-sentence purpose statement and a list of necessary actions to reach that purpose. The first exercise defines a team's purpose. The second part is to acknowledge the relevant behaviors. Although they go together, they can be split into two separate exercises.

## Where the Rubber Meets the Road

*A Purpose is like a Coat Hanger*

A purpose statement is like a coat hanger in a closet. We all have too many coat hangers, right? They seem to breed!

Coat hangers are useless on their own—they can even be downright annoying. No one pays too much attention to the humble coat hanger, and they take up too much space among our clothes.

However, the coat hanger has a purpose—it's very useful for hanging garments off. What's more, the coat hanger helps to shape the item of clothing hanging from it.

This is also the reason for a team purpose statement. Ideally, everything that's said, done, and thought about in a team should be consistent with its core purpose.

The way we approach work, the way we treat each other and our important stakeholders and customers, the way we problem-solve, the way we reward each other, the way we measure our success, and so on should reflect the team's purpose statement.

A purpose statement is an indispensable and underrated tool that guides and informs every decision made in the team (Baker 2015).[3]

Begin by asking each team member to reflect on these questions:

- What is the role of our team?
- What is our main goal?
- What benefits do we bring to our end users or customers?
- How do we define success?

Individually, people consider these questions in preparation for a team meeting. Coming to the meeting prepared enriches the team conversation. Giving people time to contemplate these questions will improve team dialog, in other words. Send the questions several days before the designated team meeting.

You need everyone involved and participating at the team meeting. Some may initially see this as a frivolous, time wasting activity. That's understandable. But hold the line. Persevere.

Begin the meeting inviting everyone to share their thought and ideas on these questions. Record this information. After everyone has shared their responses, the foundations have been laid to produce a compelling team purpose statement. This process is much better than simply asking: *What's our purpose?*

Time now to consider the ingredients of a good purpose statement. Here are some purpose statements from well-known companies:

*Build the best product, cause no unnecessary harm, use business to inspire and implement solutions to the environmental crisis.* (Patagonia)

*The Earth's most customer-centric company, where customers can find and discover anything they might want to buy online.* (Amazon)

*To ensure the ability of the earth to nurture life in all its diversity.* (Greenpeace)

*To give people the power to share and make the world more open and connected.* (Facebook)

*To organize the world's information and make it universally accessible and useful.* (Google)

Share these examples with the team—they illustrate what a dynamic purpose statement looks like.

In summary, a good purpose statement is

- Inspirational
- Expressed in a single sentence

- Focused on one key driver
- Concentrated on the end user
- Created collaboratively

Let's briefly consider each element.

*Inspirational:* The statement should be inspiring, motivating, and uplifting.

*We provide good services to our internal customers.*
The above statement is lackluster and unlikely to rouse team members to higher performance.

*Short:* As well as inspirational, a purpose statement should be brief. Purpose statements that are a paragraph or page long aren't read, let alone internalized by those it serves—or anyone else. One sentence is enough; it forces you to get to the point; it gets to the crux of what your team aspires to.

*Key driver:* Inspiring and brief, a purpose should also focus on one driver. In the examples I shared previously, you'll notice words and phrases like *best product, customer-centric, power to share,* and *universally accessible.* One key driver condenses all the blood, sweat, and tiers of team activity down to a single focal point.

*End user:* The statement—aside from being inspirational, brief, and focused on one focal point—should acknowledge the end user of the team's service or product. Who does the team help? Is it a select group of external customers or stakeholders? Is it an internal customer? Or both?

By recognizing the "customer," the statement is mindful of the impact the team's decisions have on the end user. What are the needs of the customer? And how best can the team fulfill those needs? Is it speed? Is it precision? Is it value for money? Is it timeliness? Is it quality?

*Collaborative:* And finally, the purpose statement should be created collaboratively. Everyone must have a stake in its creation—it's a team effort. If it's constructed by the leader—which is often the case—they will undoubtedly be sold on the statement. But … no one else will probably be as excited and enthusiastic about it, no matter how great it is. To be relevant and enabling, the purpose statement must be *owned* by the team.

After discussing the responses to the four questions I posed earlier, ask each person to write their version of the team's purpose, mindful of the elements I've covered. By involving everyone in producing a purpose statement, one or two team members don't dominate the process.

To illustrate how this works, if you have eight members of the team, including you as team leader, eight statements are produced initially. Don't panic; it may appear nightmarish to merge eight individual statements into one overall statement. This may seem even more problematic when there's a wide variety of viewpoints. Relax. Remember this: It will be more chaotic and time-consuming trying to create one statement from scratch. Stay with me. I've found that the following approach works wonders at arriving to a single purpose statement that everyone has a stake in.

Once individuals have crafted their version of the purpose statement, they pair up. Each person in pairs shares their statement with their partner. Together, they devise a statement that combines the best of both individual's contribution. The aim here is to end up with one statement that both people are satisfied with.

For example, here is an example of one statement:

To provide quality building materials to assist our customers to make the best structures.

And the other one:

Being efficient and speedy in our product delivery.

A possible combined statement may look like this:

Providing quality building materials efficiently and fast to assist our customers to make the best structures.

The joint statement takes the best from both contributions. This new statement is reflective of the thoughts of the two team members, in other words. Occasionally, one team member may be genuinely happy to adopt their colleague's idea without wanting to make any changes. They may feel that the other statement captures their sentiments too. This is acceptable since both people have had an input and finally agreeing that one contribution is suitable.

To summarize, using the example of a team of eight, you initially break up into four groups of two. Once these four pairs have come up with a joint declaration, you have whittled the purpose statement down to four contributions. In the case of odd numbers, one group of three is acceptable. Four people then share and discuss two statements. From this discussion, the aim is to end up with one purpose statement four team members are supportive of.

Once you have two statements, the team convenes and works with the two remaining ideas to come up with one overall purpose statement. You'll be pleasantly surprised how well this collaboration works. Ultimately, your team will arrive at a purpose statement that everyone is invested in.

The wordsmithing part of this exercise is important. Finessing the language guarantees that the final words reflect the elements of a good purpose statement. Words do shape worlds.[4]

Take a breath and reflect. You have achieved a critical step in unifying the team with a single purpose. Congratulations.

By working together in this exercise, team members have exchanged information and shared their perspectives. Since everyone had a hand in its development, the team will be fully committed to *their* purpose statement. With greater clarity, the statement inspires team members to act proactively in pursuit of its purpose—a purpose they've all bought into. The leader and members are in unison about the team's intent.

### Creating a Behavior Agreement

Creating a purpose statement is a good start. In the next step, you'll run a similar process to identify the attitudes and behaviors that support the team's purpose. This exercise takes it a step further in pinpointing the actions needed.

What are the behaviors necessary to achieve the team's purpose? Without certain actions, all you have is a few words on a piece of paper, as important as they are. Nothing changes unless the team's behaviors are consistent with the purpose statement. If behaviors aren't aligned with purpose, then a purpose statement—even with the warm glow of team collaboration—will be fruitless. Furthermore, if people's actions and purpose are incongruent, people are entitled to be cynical about purpose statements and their relevance. That's why this next step is critical.

There's a difference between attitude and behavior. An attitude is a state of mind, such as *professionalism* and *cooperation*. A behavior is a tangible manifestation of an attitude. It is important to explain this distinction to your people.

How is *professionalism* (attitude) practiced (behavior), for instance? Two behaviors that support professionalism are *following through* on promises to each other and *proofreading* reports before sending them out to customers, for example. Here is another illustration: How is *cooperation* (attitude) expressed as a tangible behavior? For *cooperation*, two supporting behaviors are *frequently asking colleagues* if they need assistance and *speaking directly* to the person with whom they may have a problem in the first instance. Behaviors that are consistent with an attitude make that attitude practical.

Team members pair up again and select two attitudes consistent with the team's purpose statement. For example, consider the purpose we used earlier:

Providing quality building materials efficiently and fast to assist our customers to make the best structures.

Two relevant attitudes supporting this purpose are *professionalism* and *responsiveness*.

Once pairs have agreed on two attitudes that support the purpose, invite them to share their response with the rest of the team. Encourage discussion on the attitudes shared.

Use these questions to facilitate the discussion on each attitude and supporting behaviors:

- How do you define this attitude?
- What should we do if this attitude has been breached?
- What behaviors are consistent with this attitude?
- How can this behavior be applied in our work and interactions?

- What is the observable evidence that this behavior has been performed?
- How does this behavior help accomplish our team's purpose?
- If this behavior is neglected, what are the consequences?

Discuss these questions with your team. They help to exchange information on the attitudes and behaviors needed to achieve the team's purpose. After these discussions, you have formulated a purpose statement and behavior agreement. The final step is to document this information for future reference.

Put them up as a poster (or several posters) around the work area to remind team members of their purpose and how it will be accomplished. Give regular feedback based on this document; in particular, reinforce when team members use their enterprising qualities consistent with the agreement. This purpose statement should also be used to affirm when your team is on the right track. Invite your colleagues to evaluate their behavior and others, based on the agreement. Done properly, these two exercises will open opportunities for people to act proactively in the interest of reaching the team's purpose.

In summary, the purpose statement and the accompanying behavior agreement give people a framework for using their independent judgment in the work they do. One of the main reasons jobholders balk at displaying their initiative is a lack of clarity around what is expected of them in their job. These structured team discussions and their outcomes open the channels of communication between everyone in the team. Through an open exchange of information, an alignment of common understanding is established. People will consequently feel psychologically safer to act proactively.

In the next chapter, we consider some practices for using the strategy of proactive accountability.

# Top 10 Points

1. Information exchange is a strategy that aims to open the communication channels between a manager and employee.

2. Two practices suitable for this strategy are a creating a team purpose statement and behavior agreement.

3. The two practices work in tandem.

4. The outcome is a one-sentence purpose statement and a list of necessary actions required to reach that purpose.

5. A good purpose statement is inspirational, expressed in one sentence, focused on one key driver, concentrated on the end user, and created collaboratively.

6. By creating a purpose statement, you have achieved a critical step in unifying the team with a single purpose.

7. In the next step, you'll run a similar process to identify the attitudes and behaviors that support the team purpose.

8. If behaviors aren't aligned with purpose, then a purpose statement—even with the warm glow of team collaboration—will be fruitless.

9. Put the team purpose statement and behavior agreement up as a poster (or several posters) around the work area to remind team members of their purpose and how it will be accomplished.

10. The purpose statement and the accompanying behavior agreement give people a framework for using their independent judgment in the work they do.

# CHAPTER 10

# Proactive Accountability Practices

Inspiring people to back their judgment and not to be completely dependent on them is one of the hallmarks of a collaborative leader.

> *Arlene Zalayet, an executive at Liberty Mutual who has 1,800 employees in her department, recently began holding 18 check-ins a month by video with groups, including entry-level workers. In one of these town halls, an administrative worker shared how Covid-19 was affecting her African-American community, sparking an important discussion about the value of the company's diversity efforts and what it would take to support different kinds of workers through this crisis (Gardner and Matviak 2020).[1]*

The strategy of proactive accountability is based on an understanding that employees can exercise their initiative and judgment in certain circumstances. But when they do act proactively, the employee does so at their own risk, with potential career consequences if the results of their actions are considered unacceptable. Proactive accountability acknowledges that in exceptional circumstances, employee initiative is warranted.

This strategy is typically suited to bureaucratic and authority-focused organizations, such as government agencies and military and paramilitary units. In these types of organizations, there is typically a clear chain of command for making decisions. In rare situations, without management endorsement, independent judgment is required, such as in a crisis or when ethical or unlawful behavior is witnessed. But if an employee acts proactively and makes a poor decision or abuses or manipulates a situation, their choice to act without management consent will be held against them.

Faced with unethical or unlawful behavior, it is reasonable—both legally and morally—for someone observing these types of actions to report this wrongdoing. Reporting this misconduct is appropriate, not only when the employee is the subject of this offense but also when they see it occurring elsewhere. By the same token, organizations don't want employees abusing this responsibility for personal gain. Taking initiative may also be justified during a crisis. Following standard protocols in extraordinary circumstances is not always suitable. But again, proactive accountability requires the employee to use their judgment wisely. Showing prudent initiative in exceptional circumstances is in the interests of the individual and the organization.

We consider two conditions and relevant practices when proactive accountability is applicable:

- Addressing unethical behavior
- Crisis management

## Addressing Unethical Behavior

While unethical behavior may not necessarily be illegal activity, it can have serious consequences for the workplace, if unaddressed. Unethical behavior creates a toxic work environment where everyone suffers, including the organization. So leaders should welcome employees responding early when they see any unethical behavior. Stopping misconduct is everyone's responsibility.

Ethical behavior, simply put, is doing the right thing. Unethical behavior is the opposite; that is doing the wrong thing. Unethical behavior includes breaking the law, such as stealing or acting violently, and lesser offenses that may not be unlawful. Misconduct occurs in all industries and organizations in many ways. Some common forms of unethical behavior include the following:

- Misusing company time
- Abusive behavior
- Theft
- Lying
- Violating company Internet policies

Misbehavior can't always be detected by management. Managers themselves may be indulging in these sorts of wrongdoings. Understandably, when an employee witnesses any of these activities, or on the receiving end, they often feel reluctant to report this, fearing the potential repercussions. And the poor behaviors—going unnoticed or unreported—fester and cause serious damage to people and the organization and its reputation. What's more, going undetected or unchecked, this tacitly emboldens more of this and other types of misbehavior. Encouraging employees to raise these incidents correctly is undoubtedly in everybody's best interests, except the offender. The challenge then is: *How can organizations encourage employees to speak up about unethical behavior without taking a risk and suffering negative repercussions?*

The authors of *Crucial Accountability: Tools for Resolving Violated Expectations, Broken Commitments, and Bad Behavior* (Patterson, Grenny, Maxfield, and Switzler 2013)[2] surveyed more than 900 employees. They found that the three most common unethical workplace behaviors identified were taking credit for someone else's work, indulging in extra-long breaks, and calling in sick when healthy. One third of the respondents reported having witnessed at least one of these violations the week prior to participating the survey. Although these misbehaviors are not unlawful, they can be detrimental, if not addressed.

Although 63 percent of the survey respondents witnessed one or more of these unethical behaviors, only half these misdeeds were reported. When survey participants were asked the reason why they weren't reported, four main reasons were cited:

- It might be damaging to career.
- It would result in making the offender harder to work with.
- The complaint wouldn't be taken seriously.
- Uncertain how to raise the matter.

In large organizations, an HR department provides a process for employees to voice their concerns about unethical behavior. HR departments also support their workforce with policies, procedures, and training. However, small businesses have few resources and little or no HR support. Small businesses don't necessarily have a clearly defined avenue for reporting or disclosing unethical behavior. Also, in these small-to-medium enterprises (SMEs), putting in place the proper guidance for addressing such behavior is usually more challenging. Urging employees to proactively report unethical behavior is difficult without a proper system in place. And if this behavior goes unaddressed, the misconduct may continue.

If your business lacks robust HR support, employees need to have a pathway for reporting their concerns. The pathway consists of a policy, a reporting process, and ethical behavior training. This takes time and money. However, managers in smaller firms can take several easy steps to effectively address unethical behavior at work. These measures can encourage proactive accountability.

In summary, these measures include

- Creating a code of ethics
- Establish a protocol
- Enable employees
- Review the code

Let's consider each step.

### Create a Code of Ethics

Setting the right tone for proper workplace behavior begins with creating a code of ethics. The code consists of the values that are important to a business and a framework for understanding the ethical boundaries at work.

A code of ethics communicates the organization's commitment to act ethically. The code should also identify a set of specific values to govern behavior. This document should be developed collaboratively with input from all employees. The code should be visible to organizational members and the public.

Developing a code of ethics begins with a conversation involving all members of the organization. Like the team values charter, vision statement, and behavior agreement, involving others draws on their perspectives and ensures that people are on board with and committed to its intent. Be sure then to involve everyone in the process of drafting and formalizing the code of ethics.

**Where the rubber meets the road**

**Code of ethics**

Here is an example of a code of ethics (Jacobson 2018):[3]

## Establish a Protocol

The protocol for the code of conduct identifies how to report unethical behavior. This protocol must protect people's anonymity. If people know they will be identified when reporting unethical behavior, it will deter them from registering misconduct. For example, this procedure might be an anonymous ethics hotline, or a go-to person one step removed from the business and someone who is objective, fair, and impartial. If the person designated for reporting unethical conduct is a manager within the business, this can be problematic. This is particularly the case if the questionable act involves them directly or indirectly. They must be fair and impartial.

Delegating someone removed from the situation sets an expectation that the concern will be taken seriously and treated fairly. This generates trust in the firm's ability to address the matter reasonably. So, if allocating this task to a trusted person within the business isn't an option, consider finding an HR partner externally who can bring objectivity and expertise to the process.

### Enable Employees

So far, we have covered the need for a code of ethics that employees have bought into and a proper protocol. Support for reporting unethical behavior is further enhanced with the necessary know-how to identify and handle ethics violations. Ethics training improves people's understanding of what ethical behavior is, and what it isn't. Investing in a sound ethics program for all new and existing employees is likely to ensure the code is adhered to.

Ethics courses are readily available and accessible, either online or face-to-face. Continually raising awareness of ethical behavior shouldn't be neglected.

### Review the Code

Constantly reviewing the code keeps a company's ethics top-of-mind and current. Refer to the code regularly and invite employees to openly evaluate the code against the behavior they observe. Here is a good question to ask your team:

- On a scale of 1 to 10 (10 is high and 1 is low), how do you think the business is traveling in terms of being consistent with our code of ethics?

Use this question to prompt a discussion in a team meeting. The adage: *Out of sight, out of mind* is true. Refer to the code regularly to keep it alive and relevant.

Ask your trusted customers to evaluate the code too. What do they observe in their dealings with the business? Where could the business improve the code? Share the feedback with the staff. Make sure all new employees as part of their induction training receive a copy of the code. Run through it with them. This emphasizes the importance the business places on ethical behavior. First impressions count.

Consider the possible real consequences of not maintaining a code of ethics for a moment. Not developing ethical culture results in lawsuits, high turnover, low morale, and potentially the ultimate demise of the business. In Chapter 7, we discussed the importance of the leader modeling the way to create the right environment for enterprising behavior to flourish. If you don't champion the written code of ethics from the outset through your actions as a leader, it will render the document useless. Modeling the way also means establishing a workable protocol and continuously reviewing its practice. Leading by example shows others you're serious about creating a positive and ethical workplace. As we've discussed several times, actions speak louder than words. By walking the talk, you are validating the documented expectations; that is, everyone is responsible for acting ethically. It also encourages people to report unethical behavior when it is observed.

Ultimately, a commitment to high ethical standards will translate to better business processes, a happier and more secure workforce, and a more successful business.

## Crisis Management

Crises such as the Covid-19 pandemic highlight the necessity to act proactively during an emergency. During a crisis, the usual practices are no longer always relevant. There is a need for more cross-functional communication. Despite a requirement to focus on the big picture during a crisis, people tend to get fixated on their immediate area of responsibility. Crises are complex and unique. They have many moving parts and are generally resolved with unorthodox responses that adopt a holistic view of the problem.

Crises come in many forms. It might be a data breach, a failure in technology, a natural disaster, or a failed product launch, for instance. Research by Quartz Insights (2018)[4] surveyed 1,200 senior global leaders. Sixty-eight percent believed that every organization will eventually be impacted by a crisis. Yet, 75 percent of respondents thought that if a crisis is managed well, an organization can eventually emerge stronger with better decision-making processes.

Leaders often try to control a crisis with their normal operating procedures. But unusual conditions are a license to break the rules, departing temporarily from the status quo. Letting go of standard practices that slow down decision making is a good start. Breaking the rules differentiates a crisis from a business as usual. However, suspending conventional practices isn't so easy in its execution.

The anxiety generated by a crisis inevitably pushes people to be risk averse. A leader wanting to play it safe in a crisis will be less trusting of team members who want to use their independent judgment. They may be reluctant to seek out differing perspectives on resolving the problem. The pathway to the "solution" is often perceived as narrow. Leaders may discard other routes that may be more effective. They will tend to fall back on actions that have worked in the past, despite the circumstances being different.

This phenomenon is called "threat rigidity" (Straw, Sandelands, and Dutton 1981).[5] The desire to try to bring things under control can result in a go-it-alone mentality. People often focus on self-preservation as resources, such as finances, job opportunities, and supplies diminish during a crisis. Communication breaks down across an organization. Instead of being proactive, people react to the calamitous environment. But successfully resolving a crisis requires the opposite response; that is, collaborating and applying sensible independent judgment.

Risk-averse leaders, who go it alone and focused on self-preservation, set the wrong tone for their team. Employees respond by erecting walls around their tasks and push their colleagues away. In a crisis, leaders should help their team break down walls, collaborate with colleagues, share their thoughts, and reach out for assistance. These are desirable proactive behaviors at any time, but particularly in a crisis.

There are broadly three effective crisis management practices: a swift assessment of the situation, responding with agility, and suspending standard operational procedures. Everything should be open to scrutiny during crisis mode. Leaders pave the way. By their actions, they send a signal that this is not business as usual; priorities and protocols are open for change. Being agile is the new black.

If leaders are agile in times of crisis—despite this going against the grain of human nature—others will follow. Leaders need others to back their judgment (within certain parameters), rather than playing it safe and merely following conventional processes. Doing what needs to be done is the right approach. This might be as simple as consults a manager in another department without clearing this with their manager first. In calmer times, not following the clear chain-of-command may be frowned upon in a bureaucratic organization. In a crisis, however, where speed is paramount, bypassing their manager is a better response. Even so, the employee is taking a risk of breaking this convention. A good crisis manager would welcome such an initiative in the interest of speed.

Effective leaders pivot in times of crisis. This means making quick strategic decisions, adopting course corrections, reprioritizing, and removing roadblocks when they get in the way. Again, by setting the tone, these actions reassure others that it's okay to follow suit and be enterprising too.

Engaging the team is important too. Effective leaders facilitate team conversations with full participation to entertain divergent perspectives. The traditional manager, on the other hand, believes that they must always be in charge and have all the answers—or at least pretend to. Transformational leaders are humble enough to appreciate that they don't have all the answers. They know that this is especially true in times of turbulence. Enabling junior employees who demonstrate capability and commitment to make decisions is real crisis leadership. This fully utilizes the leader's pool of talent. Inspiring people to back their judgment and not to be completely dependent on them is one of the hallmarks of a collaborative leader.

Collaborative leaders remind people that achieving the right outcome takes priority over faithfully adhering to the status quo. Whether it's changing an approval process or shifting responsibilities within the team, decision making and execution need to be expedited in a crisis. Minimizing bureaucracy, being prepared to be agile, sharing accountability across the team, and sharpening response times with increased responsiveness are overriding practices. Being solution focused takes precedence over reinforcing compliance.

More than ever, in times of upheaval cultivating, a shared purpose (another proactive strategy) is not to be underestimated. A shared purpose, as we have covered, builds a positive culture and increases enterprising behavior when required. This is achieved by continually keeping team members in the loop and providing updates on new strategies and developments. Leaders can develop a culture based on a shared purpose through regular communication. People can then understand and appreciate why strategies and priorities frequently change and how their roles can adapt to meet these adjustments.

As well as communicating shifts in priorities in times of crisis, it is important to reinforce the overall objective too. A belief that the work people do helps to resolve the crisis inspires them to think and act as a team and be more open to collaborating. Communicating the overall objective lowers people's uncertainty and boosts their confidence to reach out to their colleagues in uncertain times.

When executed properly, crisis management often—and sometimes surprisingly—brings out the best in people and improves the business. Crises can, for instance, unearth new business opportunities and people gain new skills and capabilities. These benefits can be implemented postcrisis.

Whether employees are prepared to exercise proactive accountability largely depends on their level of trust. Encouraging people to ask naïve questions and constructively challenge strategies is a good starting point to build trust in the team environment. Collaboration also means involving people in tackling novel and complicated problems. Through group problem-solving—although time-consuming—potential risks and solutions can be discussed that may elude individual experts.

It's not only your immediate team that you need to communicate within times of crisis. Connect with the frontline employees too. Being accessible to people directly liaising with customers gives the leader unfiltered information about people's actions and thoughts. Talking regularly with frontline workers is especially critical when people are working remotely. This taps into their ideas, and by bringing them into the tent, it supports them to use their enterprising qualities.

Getting team members to reflect on their preferred way of working is also useful to promote enterprising behavior. When under pressure, people retreat to their comfort zone. It's helpful therefore to understand what kinds of behaviors come naturally, both of oneself and those they work with. For instance, when pressure builds, do you prefer to dive into the details or stand back and appreciate the big picture? As team members become more aware of their colleague's natural behavioral styles, they can figure out how to use these tendencies to work more effectively together. Revisit your team's behavior types if this is something you have done in the past.

Play to your strengths. Instead of trying to change your natural tendencies—which is almost impossible to sustain during the stress of a crisis—focus instead on consciously using your innate style to improve collective decision making. If you are naturally drawn to teamwork, then use your enthusiasm to foster an esprit de corps, for example. Harnessing innate talents makes sense in a time of turbulence.

Crises like the Covid-19 pandemic highlight the importance of breaking the rules (or creating new ones), being outcome focused, and agile. These factors can be promoted by using a collaborative leadership style rather than an autocratic approach. By using a collective approach to problem-solving, it inspires people to be proactive. Proactive accountability is a suitable strategy in times of crisis to break the proactive paradox.

That completes Part II. We have explored several practices that are consistent with the framework. Hopefully, this stimulates your imagination to try new ways of encouraging more initiative in your team. In Part III, we consider the second dimension of promoting independent judgment—the job itself.

# Top 10 Points

1. The strategy of proactive accountability is based on an understanding that employees can exercise their initiative and judgment in certain circumstances.
2. Addressing unethical behavior and crisis management are two areas suitable for adopting the proactive accountability strategy.
3. To encourage proactive accountability in reporting unethical behavior is easier with a code of ethics, an established protocol, training employees, and reviewing the code.
4. Setting the right tone for proper workplace behavior begins with creating a code of ethics.
5. The protocol for the code of conduct identifies how to report unethical behavior.
6. Ethics training improves people's understanding of what ethical behavior is, and what it isn't. Investing in a sound ethics program for all new and existing employees is likely to ensure the code is adhered to.

7. Constantly reviewing the code keeps a company's ethics top-of-mind and current.

8. Crises such as the Covid-19 pandemic highlight the necessity to act proactively during an emergency.

9. Leaders often try to control a crisis with their normal operating procedures. But unusual conditions are a license to break the rules, departing temporarily from the status quo.

10. There are broadly three effective crisis management practices: a swift assessment of the situation, responding with agility, and suspending standard operational procedures.

# PART III

# Job Design

# CHAPTER 11

# Rethinking Job Design

Although the work we do has changed dramatically since the early days
of the Ford assembly line, the way work is designed hasn't changed.

*Barbara is a business unit leader overwhelmed by the amount of time
she spends making decisions: hiring decisions for managers several levels below her, signoffs on small business expenses, and minor changes
to operating procedures. She never has time to think about strategic
decisions.*

*Barbara decided to be more adamant about delegating decisions to
her direct reports. Within days, problems arose, and she thought some
of the decisions made were poor. Sticking to her guns, she did not take
back the decisions, but gave clear feedback and held them accountable. But she realized many decisions still waited for her informal
endorsement, so they weren't necessarily moving faster, even in the
cases where people made the right decisions without her. Her team
continuously found creative ways to ask her to make the decision. As
meetings and committees piled up, particularly one-on-one "check-
ins," she realized she was being tested by her team for what the "right"
decision was. Her goal of more accountability and faster decisions
seemed to be going in the wrong direction, despite her best attempts to
empower people (De Smet, Hewes, and Weiss 2020).[1]*

So far, we have defined the proactive paradox and its origins in Part I. In
Part II, we have considered four strategies for breaking the paradox and
how and when each approach should be applied. Specifically, we have
discussed several different practices relevant to shared purpose, boundary
management, information exchange, and proactive accountability. In Part
III, we ponder the job itself and how this can be a potential source of

stimulating employee initiative. Job design has been a major—and generally overlooked—stumbling block to developing an environment for positive proactive behavior to flourish.

The concept of job crafting is an approach that can augment traditional job design. I consider what it is and how it can be applied. Specifically, job crafting in its current form is extended to cultivating nonjob roles and using employees' strengths and talents.

We shift the emphasis in Part III from situations and circumstances suited to apply each of the four strategies to job design.

The central question I want to address is: *How can an employee change their job, with the support of their manager, to foster appropriate initiative and productive independent judgment?*

In this chapter, I want to begin with a critique of conventional job design that has largely been unchanged for over a century. Job specification is the essence of job design. It should be acknowledged that job specification has served industry well for much of that time. But this form of job design is becoming increasingly inefficient in a climate of accelerated change and uncertainty. I will explain why this is the case.

We've all seen the engagement survey results. Most people are disengaged in their work. Some surveys suggest that 70 percent of people don't like their job (Gallo 2011).[2] Leadership books and workshops have sprouted an array of strategies and techniques designed to extract more from people at work. These concepts and fads have had limited success on improving engagement levels. This raises two important questions: *If these tactics aren't successful, why not? And what else can be done to boost engagement and meaning in the work employees do?*

The popular methods in the leadership development industry focus on changing people, not the work they do. The idea of redesigning work, or at least making it more attractive, is usually bypassed. Applying "empowerment" leadership tactics to change people isn't working. The assumption is that that the way jobs are structured is not the problem, it's the people and the way they are lead. I believe it's time for a rethink about the job itself and how it's designed. Job design holds one of the keys to unlocking enterprise, engagement, and accountability.

Furthermore, the two big gaps in conventional leadership development are the lack of attention on two workplace relationships. One is the working relationship between the employee and the manager. We explored the employment relationship in Part I and how it is shaped by the psychological contract. The other relationship is the one between the jobholder and their job. We now turn our attention to that relationship. Like the employment relationship, how jobs are designed is sidestepped as a source for realizing the true potential of people at work.

The stumbling block is that the way jobs are designed is outdated in responding to the changing world of work. Current job design has its origins in scientific management that originated over 100 years ago.

Job specification, the main principle of job design, began with management consultant Frederick Taylor's scientific management philosophy. Taylor broke the Ford Motor Company assembly line up into a series of specified tasks. He subsequently analyzed each component separately to determine how performing those tasks could be carried out most efficiently.

The driver for job specification was efficiency and waste minimization. By identifying the "one best way" of performing each task, wastage in time, effort, and resources are abated. Taylor studied each job in the factory to determine the least amount of time and effort required to complete it to a high standard. Standardized methods of performing each task were documented. Each job on the assembly line would be meticulously planned. Jobholders were trained to carry out tasks in a specified way; they were then paid to perform tasks in the way stipulated by management.

Today's job specifications originated from Taylorism. A job specification entails breaking down a job into its simplest parts. The job, with clear specifications, is then assigned to a trained jobholder to perform each task consistently and efficiently. Although the work we do has changed dramatically since the early days of the Ford assembly line, the way work is designed hasn't changed.

There are several advantages to designing work around a job specification. Breaking tasks into small easy-to-manage elements, with clearly defined repetitive processes, lessens the skill requirement of the job itself. Job specification also decreases any discretionary effort in doing the tasks—including being creative and displaying initiative. This reduces costs. Training is standardized and comes from a procedure manual.

Recurring tasks are broken into simple parts that are easy to learn and getting people skilled up is quick and cost-effective.

But job specification has its drawbacks. From a motivational perspective, breaking a job into small, monotonous, and simple parts can make work dull and monotonous. There is little room for creative thinking and variety. Boredom doing simple, repetitive tasks leads to negative consequences, like high levels of absenteeism. Job specification is ineffectual and even counterproductive in a VUCA environment. In a volatile marketplace—which is now the norm—the workforce needs to continually adjust its approach in anticipation of extraordinary conditions.

Successfully producing products and services in a competitive and ever-changing environment requires agility and ingenuity. This agile approach can't be generically documented in a job specification or its buddy, the job description. Job specification puts the onus on the manager to be accountable for making sure people are following the plan. This deprives the jobholder of the ultimate responsibility and ownership over job output.

---

## Where the Rubber Meets the Road

*The Conflicting Psychological Contracts and the Job Description*

Travis is a manager who has beliefs consistent with a new psychological contract. He believes employees have multiple organizational roles to perform and not just confined to the bundle of tasks in the job description. Travis is open to the idea of working with his employees in a collaborative working relationship. His leadership style consequently is based on dialog with his team when the situation calls for it. Travis expects his employees to come up with suggestions for improving the flow of work, to work together as a team, to strive to improve their skills set, and to generally adopt an enthusiastic approach to their work.

However, Jerry, one of Travis's team members, has an old-fashioned attitude to the relationship between boss and worker. Jerry holds the view that it is the manager's responsibility to create the right atmosphere for the team to thrive in; it is the manager's responsibility to build the team; it is the manager's responsibility to make improvements in the working arrangements, and so on. After all, in Jerry's mind, that is what the boss gets paid to do. Furthermore, Jerry sees his role as getting on and completing the tasks on his job description; anything else is doing extra work that's not necessary. As a result of these conflicting expectations, Jerry views these nonjob roles as peripheral and a waste of time and energy. These incompatible unwritten expectations between Travis and Jerry result in some real frustration, even though both are, in their own ways, trying to accomplish what they understand to be their duty (Baker 2015).[3]

Taylor's philosophy of scientific management paved the way for automating and standardizing work, virtually universal in today's workplace. The concept of the assembly line, where each worker performs simple tasks in a recurring fashion, is still the norm. It's not just in manufacturing, job specification looms large in service industries too. One of the biggest modern-day success stories in applied scientific management is the McDonald's franchise operation. McDonald's was the first fast-food restaurant chain to incorporate the divisions of specification; one person takes the orders while someone else makes the burgers, another person applies the condiments, and yet another wraps them. With this level of efficiency, the customer is guaranteed to receive a hamburger of reliable quality and speedy service. All types of work, including professions and knowledge work, are organized around specific processes and formulas.

So, if job specification can be applied successfully in McDonald's restaurants—and now a feature of most fast-food franchise systems—how can it be problematic? Specification, as I've described it, encumbers adaptive behavior and hampers agility. Apart from being repetitive and dull—and the impact that has on motivation levels—fully engaging people is difficult. Although you don't read about it in the management books, job design explains the high levels of disengagement around the world and across all industries.

Someone who wants to be proactive is going to get frustrated quickly when confronted with an endless procession of standardized processes and procedures to follow. In a segmented and process-driven workplace, questioning the status quo isn't valued to the same extent as following the status quo. What's more, specializing in a narrow band of tasks implies that the specialist "knows best." Specialists are inclined to obediently follow established practices. If a completely new method is advanced in a procedure-driven environment, it infers the "old" system is somehow inferior or substandard. The novel idea isn't easy to accept and is seldom adopted. The established system is vigorously defended, and a proposed new way rejected, in other words.

To illustrate, consider the situation when a customer is overcharged. Rapid and reasonable response to rectifying a mistake usually requires a flexible approach from someone in the offending company. But a strict, process-driven workplace will inhibit an unorthodox reply to an error, no matter how sensible it appears. Employees—when mistakes are made—understandably default to the apparent safety of following the stock-standard approach. Innovation and continuous improvement are suppressed in a workplace segmented into clearly defined job specifications. Implying a need for improvement suggests that the established system is broken in some way and that—as I say—is difficult to accept. Job specification, therefore, undermines flexibility and agility.

But to be truly responsive to a customer's needs require agility, and being agile means using new approaches when the circumstances warrant it. Job specification breeds a paint-by-numbers mentality: *This is how we do things. We've always done things this way. If we follow the system, we'll be successful.* These are the prevailing assumptions of the job specification. McDonald's took a long time—many would say, too long—to change direction when it introduced "healthy" food options into its menu, for example. Changing direction is tricky in a business comprised of a series of specified methods and processes.

Although a job specification is an effective way of holding a jobholder accountable for the work they're supposed to do, it's ineffective at cultivating independent judgment. Job specification breeds tunnel vision: the employee cannot understand or appreciate the way the rest of the organization operates—and doesn't necessarily want to. This blinkered thinking is designed to get the employee to focus all their energies on doing a few, manageable work tasks to a required standard.

The job description is the working document used to support the job specification. Let's consider the job description and how it's critical to job design.

The purpose of the job description is to spell out how the job specification should be interrupted by the jobholder. However, there is usually a legal disclaimer at the end of the document. Apart from carrying out the duties stated in the document, this clause says something like:

*The jobholder is required to perform any other duties assigned by the supervisor.*

This is another paradox! This legal qualification implies that the job description fails to capture *all* the work requirements the employee is expected to perform.

It's hard to imagine a worker on the assembly line of the Ford Motor Company needing this kind of legal disclaimer. In those days, jobs were extremely specific and clearly defined and the world was less litigious than it is now! What was expected of workers in those stable work settings was very task specific. Since then, the nature of work has changed profoundly. Work is now more multifaceted, the boundaries are more ambiguous, and the performance indicators are more complex. It's no longer possible to accommodate the magnitude of these changes in a job description. So instead of rethinking how work should be redesigned, we merely tag a legal rider at the bottom of the job description to cover all bases. Unsurprisingly, we see Dilbert-like jokes about the worth and value of the job description.

There are undoubtedly many challenges crafting the ideal job description. You probably know this when you consider your own job description and compare it to the work you do. I know this too, having spoken with frustrated clients across 21 industry groups. A survey by *The Creative Group* polled advertising and marketing executives on the greatest challenge they face writing job descriptions. When asked what the main problem is in formulating job descriptions, 28 percent of respondents said it was the identification of the necessary *soft* skills for the job. Twenty-four percent claimed it was most difficult to accurately describe job duties (Castellano 2014).[4] These figures illustrate the complexity of modern-day work and trying to document it.

The concept of the job specification has largely stayed the same for 100 years. Some attempts have been made to modify it to keep pace with the transformations in work. In one of my previous books, *The End of the Job Description* (Baker 2015),[5] I explain the evolution in the format of the job description. The first-generation job description was a simple list of the tasks required by the jobholder. The focus initially was basically a list of tasks that made up the job. The second-generation job description included—apart from a list of tasks—the necessary competencies required by the jobholder to do the tasks. The focus shifted somewhat from the tasks to the attributes of the jobholder. We are now entering a third-generation phase of the job description. This phase emphasizes, in addition to tasks and competencies, some of the nonjob roles expected to be performed by the jobholder. The focus is now shifting to the needs of the organization. There is a growing awareness of the roles people are expected to play at work, apart from the tasks of the job. Although slow to take hold, this is an encouraging development.

I will have more to say about the third-generation job description and in particular, the relevance of nonjob roles to empowering employees in Chapter 14.

Even though work has advanced beyond the usefulness of the job description, our reliance on it to support HR functions is increasing. The job description is used to:

- Recruit and select employees
- Manage performance
- Identify training needs and development opportunities
- Inform succession planning
- Gauge remuneration levels
- Reward employees

and other aspects of the employee's work. It is no exaggeration to say that the job description is the bedrock of all human activities in the organization.

But this increasing dependence on the job description constrains employee enterprise.

In summary, the job description centers on the tasks employees are supposed to do in their job. The structure of the job description supports the job design specifications. It is primarily focused on the jobholder's tasks and responsibilities. The task-based approach to job design has its origins in scientific management. This design is based on Frederick Taylor's notion that jobs can be studied and specified, and that work methods used for jobs should be rationalized.

In the next two chapters, we look closer at the harmful effects of the job description in stimulating the independent judgment of people at work.

## Top 10 Points

1. Job specification is the essence of job design.
2. The stumbling block is that the way jobs are designed is outdated in responding to the changing world of work.
3. The driver for job specification was efficiency and waste minimization.
4. A job specification entails breaking down a job into its simplest parts.
5. Taylor's philosophy of scientific management paved the way for automating and standardizing work, virtually universal in today's workplace.
6. Someone who wants to be proactive is going to get frustrated quickly when confronted with an endless procession of standardized processes and procedures to follow.
7. Although a job specification is an effective way of holding a jobholder accountable for the work they're supposed to do, it's ineffective at cultivating independent judgment.
8. The purpose of the job description is to spell out how the job specification should be interrupted by the jobholder.
9. Even though work has advanced beyond the usefulness of the job description, our reliance on it to support HR functions is increasing.
10. The increasing dependence on the job description constrains employee enterprise.

# CHAPTER 12

# The Job Description's Limitations for Developing People

Exposure to a broad range of learning options—besides technical training—takes into consideration the development of the *whole person* and not just in the *jobholder*.

*John sat down with Peter to conduct his dreaded annual performance appraisal; he was anxious about this interview since he had several concerns about Peter's work. He was apprehensive about Peter's reaction. There were four aspects of Peter's work that John wanted to discuss. These areas are Peter's lack of initiative, his poor interpersonal relationships with colleagues, his lack of commitment to developing his skill set, and his generally negative attitude around the office. On the positive side, John was satisfied with Peter's technical knowhow. To overcome his apprehension, John thoroughly prepared for the interview, citing several examples.*

*As Peter took his seat, John noticed he had a copy of his job description clutched in his hands. John got straight to the point, "Peter, I think you are doing your job well in lots of areas, but there are four areas I am concerned about." "What are they?" "Well firstly, I am concerned that you don't show enough initiative in carrying out your work. For example, on Monday you complained to me that you are short-staffed. However, I noticed that you were doing tasks that you could have delegated to other people. You need to show more initiative and do things differently." "But nowhere on my job description does it mention the need to be innovative," Peter fired back.*

*After an awkward pause, John continued, "And the other day, you didn't help out in the production area when you finished your workload. That's not being a team player in my book." "It might be in your book, John, but again, being a team player is not stated in my job description anywhere."*

*"Also, I have been trying for months to get you to do that new course on report writing. You keep telling me that you've been too busy. Apart from anything else, Peter, it would help you develop your career skills." "I don't see developing my career skills written down anywhere on this job description," said Peter, looking down at the two-page document in front of him.*

*Plowing on, "I am also concerned that in the team meeting on Monday your attitude to the suggestions of others was pretty negative. I need you to display a more positive attitude toward your work colleagues." "Where is being positive and nice to people written in this document?" challenged Peter.*

*John thought to himself that these job descriptions were a waste of time. Surely there must be a better way to get Peter to focus on performance in his role (Baker 2015).[1]*

In the last chapter, I claimed that we need to rethink the way jobs are designed. We discussed the origins of the job specification and its extension, the job description. My argument for redesigning jobs is that job specification places a straitjacket on the jobholder that restricts their capacity to think for themselves. Creative thinking and independent judgment are essential attributes in the changing world of work.

In the next two chapters, I'll explain how the job description limits the jobholder's ability to be proactive. What's more, the job description influences every aspect of the employee lifecycle. These constraints illustrate the need to redesign work to boost employee empowerment.

This chapter looks at the HR practices designed to develop employees. In the next chapter, the focus is on the HR practices that reward employees.

Before looking at the three key HR practices for developing the employee, I want to briefly consider four important nonjob roles that are rarely covered in the job description.

Based on the current job specification design, performing in a job and performing at work are not the same. Put another way: You can achieve all the KRAs in the job description and still underperform. Or in reverse: You can perform at work without following the exact requirements specified in the job description. How so?

## Nonjob Roles

Nonjob roles have an increasing bearing on work performance. Nonjob roles, however, don't feature prominently, if at all, in the job description. Performing at work is more than accomplishing the tasks cited in the job description.

I will discuss nonjob roles in more depth and their relevance to performance in Chapter 14.

Here is an illustration of what I mean. Consider one's attitude. I'm sure you'd agree that a poor attitude can adversely affect job performance. Being constantly critical and chronically unenthusiastic undoubtedly saps everyone's energy. Low energy doesn't lead to high performance.

Even so, *adopting a positive attitude* isn't usually mentioned in the job description. And on the rare occasion, that attitude is stated in the document, it's expressed in general terms. For someone to be engaged and empowered involves having a positive attitude, or at least, not a poor attitude.

Here's a second example of a vital nonjob role: teamwork. What of someone choosing not to be a team player? What if they decide to not work collaboratively and constructively with their colleagues? What if they are technically skilled at their job but a pain in the backside to deal with? An unwillingness to be a team player will undoubtedly limit performance, regardless of their technical skills.

Superior technical competency won't make up for self-centered behavior at work. Despite this, *working with and through other people constructively* is not universally included in the job description; or if it is, it only gets a fleeting mention. Like attitude, teamwork—another critical nonjob role—affects people's performance.

The third illustration of an essential nonjob role is growing and developing. Daniel, for example, is an employee in an administrative position that resists learning a new computer software system introduced in his company. He decides to continue using the old software, even when the new program is quicker. The reluctance of Daniel to learn to use a new system slows him down. Furthermore, Daniel's stubbornness slows down operations in his team. We all know people like Daniel—people who are unwilling to embrace new learning opportunities. An aversion to up-skill harms productivity.

Being in a constant state of learning and professional growth is an asset to the organization. Like the other two nonjob roles I flagged, the job description rarely refers to *continuous learning and growth*. Yet again it's integral to individual and organizational success.

One more illustration of a nonjob role: innovation and continuous improvement. Consider Jeanette who believes that *if it ain't broke, don't fix it*. She upholds the view that *this is the way we have always done things around here*. These clichés are common in workplaces. But to prosper and progress in an ever-changing environment, we need constant renewal.

Innovation and continuous improvement are the antidotes in a rapidly changing world. Offering constructive suggestions for improvement—or at least being willing to try new approaches—is necessary to stay relevant. *How can things be done faster/with less effort/in less time/with less cost/with more effect/with greater impact/in safer ways?* are questions enterprising employees ask, or at least think about.

Although *innovation and continuous improvement* is a common phrase, it's not common practice. We wait despairingly for Peter Senge's *learning organization* to materialize (Senge 1990),[2] some 30 years since he wrote about it! Building a learning organization is beyond the scope of this book. Nonetheless, its elusiveness shouldn't be a deterrent to empowering all jobholders from being part of the discussion on making the workplace more efficient and effective. People who are closed to sensible new approaches to work, or worse—sabotaging other's wanting to try new approaches—strangle progress. Being receptive to new approaches and offering suggestions for improvement are a catalyst for better performance.

If continuous improvement (and innovation) is stated in the job description, it's expressed in vague terms like: *The jobholder needs to demonstrate a willingness to be flexible and innovative*. It's a fuzzy statement that's probably not going to be taken seriously by the jobholder. Until a crisis hits the business, workplace improvement is often put on the backburner. If it's not featured prominently in the job description, the jobholder is off the hook; there is no pressure for them to challenge the status quo.

When these four nonjob roles are fully exercised, they positively impact performance. So, why aren't they expressed explicitly in the job description? Even though KRAs are stated in detail, with no reference to nonjob roles render the job description incomplete—and therefore deficient. Without any emphasis on nonjob roles employees are expected to play, the job description doesn't spell out the totality of work performance.

More about this is discussed in Chapter 14.

## The Employee Lifecycle

I want to now turn to the six key HR practices that affect all employees. Furthermore, I want to illustrate the omnipotence of the job description, present in all these practices.

Figure 12.1 illustrates six-core HR practices in the employee's organizational life cycle.

In Figure 12.1, you can see the six primary HR practices that the employee is exposed to during their employment lifecycle. The first three practices (*recruitment and selection*, *induction and onboarding*, and *training and development*) broadly involve the employee's development. The other three practices (*remuneration and rewarding*, *promoting and planning succession*, and *appraising and reviewing*) are associated with rewarding employees. Although the six practices have a bearing on each other, I will, however, discuss each separately and in the order illustrated. More specifically, I'll discuss the influence the job description has on each practice. This will highlight the prominence of the job description and how job design hinders the empowerment of the people at work.

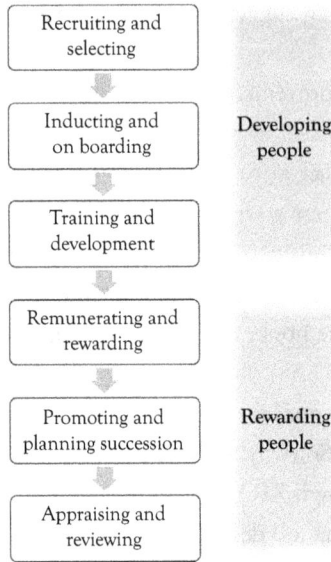

Figure 12.1 *The employee lifecycle*

## Recruiting and Selecting

Unless it's an internal appointment, the first contact an employee has with the organization is during the selection process, typically in an interview. The normal method for selecting the best candidate is done by matching their experience and qualifications with job-related requirements. There's universal acceptance that the best criterion for selecting the *right* employee is based on the job's competencies.

At first glance, this method seems perfectly valid, fair, and reliable. It seems a very rational process to match the candidate with a specific job vacancy. But the process is too dependent on the job's task-related competencies to select candidates, at the expense of other attributes. Managers typically look for the person with the closest skills-set fit, based on "best practice." Other considerations are peripheral.

Nonjob roles aren't considered to the same extent in the recruitment and selection process. And on the rare occasion when they are counted, the nonjob dimension isn't judged with the same scrutiny as that used to assess job competencies.

Once several candidates match the job-specific criteria, they are shortlisted for an interview. During the interview, the selection panel asks each candidate the same set of questions based on the job specification. The contender with the highest ratings for the job-specific criteria usually gets an offer to fill the position. In short, the person judged to have the best experience and mastery that matches the job specification usually gets the job.

But attributes such as

- Attitude and enthusiasm
- The ability to work constructively with a variety of colleagues and stakeholders
- Readiness to develop personally and technically and
- Preparedness to question the status quo

are secondary considerations.

Despite the bias toward technical competence, the selection panel understands the significance of these attributes for success. The panel may make some assumptions about the candidate's capacity to fulfill these nonjob attributes. But it's usually only fleeting guesswork. The selection panel is pressured by HR to focus its attention on technical skills and qualifications.

This first practice diminishes the status of nonjob roles in the selection process, even though we know these attributes impact work performance. It's only after several weeks or months on the job that it becomes apparent whether the recruit contributes beyond their job obligations.

---

## Where the Rubber Meets the Road

### If Only We Knew ...

After the probationary period lapsed, Lisa—one of the selection panelists—turns to Rod, another on the panel, and says, with a rueful expression three months later, "If only we had known when we interviewed Bill (the new employee) several months ago that he would treat everyone with contempt and disrespect." "If only!" repeats Rod with a sigh.

So, nonjob attributes aren't assessed thoroughly, if at all, during the selection process, despite them having a major bearing on performance. By evaluating a candidate's worth solely on the confines of a job specification, organizations aren't allowing for a broader interpretation of work performance. The lens for recruitment and selection is based on the job description—and little else—unfortunately.

By undervaluing nonjob roles at the outset of one's employment lifecycle, it sends a signal to a new employee that exercising nonjob behaviors are less important than fulfilling the task requirements in the job description.

### Inducting and Onboarding

Once the selection ritual is over, the employee commences their new job. Most new employees—particularly those recruited from outside the organization—are a mix of excitement and apprehension on day one. The starting employee is eager to learn and absorb new information. This early stage in the employment lifecycle is a golden opportunity to positively shape and mold expectations. It's a good opportunity to break old, unhelpful habits. Leaders generally understand the value of a well-run induction program for new employees.

A thorough induction program includes a mix of information and training. Training is usually a combination of formal or informal learning. The focus is primarily on the new job requirements. During this early stage of employment, the leader can share their expectations, including nonjob roles and responsibilities.

A collaborative leader will use the induction period to discuss their expectations beyond the job specification. Being impressionable at this stage of a new job, the new employee is likely to be probably receptive to the leader's standards and expectations. The recruit also has a set of expectations about their new boss. As we've discussed earlier, the manager and employee's views aren't always in sync; they may have different psychological contracts. The induction process is a good place to start discussing differences in outlook if they exist. Discussing nonjob roles and expectations can unearth beliefs that may prove problematic later in the relationship. But alas, this conversation doesn't take place often, even in the early stages of the employment relationship.

Instead, the early interactions between the recruit and their new boss center mostly on the tasks of the job. A job focus during onboarding further entrenches the idea that nonjob attributes aren't as relevant as the specifications of the job.

## Training and Development

Once the probationary period passes, the employee is offered training opportunities to develop their skills on the job. Although nonjob training opportunities, such as team development and communication, are more prevalent than they once were, they are less prominent than job-specific training.

Training for job skills mastery is still the mainstay of employee development; this hasn't changed since the birth of industry. Improving job skills is undeniably important. But to succeed in a rapidly changing marketplace, as stated before, needs more than superior technical skills.

People in all industries are continually bombarded with one-off challenges that can't be addressed by applying standardized technical skills. The solution to fixing a "wicked problem"[3] isn't usually found in the company manual or solved by technical training. Complex problem-solving needs sound independent judgment.

The empowered employee benefits from a variety of learning methods, including both technical and nontechnical knowledge. Exposure to a broad range of learning options—besides technical training—takes into consideration the development of the *whole person* and not just in the *jobholder*. But with the job description's strong focus on task-related accomplishment, it's harder to justify spending money on nonjob training opportunities.

A hypercompetitive and unpredictable marketplace presents unique and challenging problems, as I've said several times. Applying one's initiative and independent judgment—often on the spur of the moment—is paramount in coping with fluctuations and uncertainty at work. Furthermore, many of the attributes necessary to work in a VUCA world are beyond the scope of the job description. Being adaptive and enterprising can be as valuable as one's technical capabilities. Today's workforce needs a wider set of attributes than those contained within the job description.

In the next chapter, we will consider the next three HR practices that relate to rewarding employees.

# Top 10 Points

1. Based on the current job specification design, performing in a job and performing at work are not the same.
2. Nonjob roles have an increasing bearing on work performance.
3. When nonjob roles are fully exercised, they positively impact performance.
4. Without any emphasis on nonjob roles that employees are expected to play, the job description doesn't spell out the totality of work performance.
5. Even when the task requirements are expressed in detail, no reference to nonjob roles mean the job description is incomplete, and therefore deficient.
6. The six core HR practices in the employee's organizational life cycle are recruiting and selecting, inducting and onboarding, training and development, remunerating and rewarding, promoting and planning succession, and appraising and reviewing.
7. The recruitment process diminishes the status of nonjob roles in the selection process.
8. In the induction and onboarding phase, the early interactions between the recruit and their new boss center mostly on the tasks of the job.
9. Once the probationary period passes, the employee is offered training opportunities to develop their skills on the job.
10. Many of the attributes necessary to work in a VUCA world are beyond the scope of the job description.

# CHAPTER 13

# The Job Description's Limitations for Rewarding People

*From entry to exit, the job description is ubiquitous in the life of an employee.*

*Jeanette is an HR manager with a traditional outlook. Her training budget is almost entirely spent on technical training. Jeanette expects employees to learn, follow, and be accountable for sticking to the literal requirements of their job description. She judges success by how compliant people are in following the company's systems and processes. When a dilemma arises, Jeanette wants employees to refer to the comprehensive procedures manual she calls "The Bible."*

*She could be described as a transactional leader. Managers in her opinion are there to lead and make decisions. Jeanette's paperwork is impeccably completed, and she believes in compliance and risk aversion. She is hands-on and has a reputation for burying herself in the detail of an issue.*

*Jeanette thinks good training is following and getting through the training workbook before the end of the time allotted. Training is usually done formally in a classroom with a trainer referring to a set training manual.*

*Craig replaced her as the HR manager and has an entirely different learning and development philosophy. He changed the name of the department to "People, Performance, and Well-being." Craig changed the training agenda and introduced such courses as lateral thinking and problem-solving; he places more emphasis on personal development.*

*Unlike Jeanette, Craig believes his role is to transform the organiza-*
*tion's culture to become an employer of choice. He leaves operational*
*matters to line managers, who Craig believes are in the best position to*
*deal with day-to-day issues. Much to the frustration of several train-*
*ing consultants who had a good working relationship with Craig's*
*predecessor, they're asked by Craig to shorten their sessions and break*
*the program into smaller chunks. The trainers were used to coming in*
*and running one-day programs. He spent his first few weeks talking*
*to employees to hear their thoughts. Craig wanted to understand the*
*challenges they faced in their jobs (Baker 2014).[1]*

In this chapter, we continue the journey through the employee lifecycle. Previously, I outlined the six main HR practices in the lifecycle and
explained the first three functions. These three practices are recruiting
and selecting, inducting and onboarding, and training and development.
Each practice—with its dependency on the job description—limits people's growth to their job task obligations. The priority is developing the
jobholder before the person.

Now let's look at next three HR practices in the employee lifecycle. These procedures are about rewarding people, namely, remunerating and rewarding, promoting and planning succession, and appraising
and reviewing. The pattern of overdependence on the job description
continues.

## Remunerating and Rewarding

Assessing employees' pay levels fairly isn't easy, regardless of the method
used. Managers rely heavily on the job description to inform their decisions on pay rises. Awarding or rejecting a pay raise is achieved by measuring the jobholder against their job specification. This is done under
the guise of fairness and impartiality. Using other criteria, apart from the
job description, is usually not considered. Straying outside the jobholder's role in making remuneration decisions is perceived as too subjective.
So, pay level assessments center on assessing the jobholder's performance
against the key performance indicators (KPIs) in the job description.
What's more, it's standard practice to pay people doing the same job,

with the same job description—regardless of their performance—the same wage.

Using other indicators, apart from KPIs in the job description, leaves a manager open to charges of bias. Yet, whatever the criteria, being completely objective about assessing people's value at work, isn't possible. Our belief of being a rational and objective decision maker is misguided. Human beings are prone—far more than we'd like to believe—to bias in virtually everything we judge. Managers delude themselves into thinking they make rational and logical decisions. But it's a fallacy.

Based on this erroneous belief of being an objective decision maker, the attraction of measuring performance against KPIs is plausible, at least on the surface. Accounting for other factors in remuneration decisions—such as nonjob performance—is perceived as too subjective. Nonjob attributes are therefore peripheral in rewarding employees. Nonjob contributions such as the following:

- One's attitude and enthusiasm
- The ability to work in a team
- A readiness to develop oneself
- Contributing to the efficiency and effectiveness of the workplace

are bypassed. These enterprising qualities aren't considered in remuneration decisions.

Therefore, the manager doesn't raise these attributes during the remuneration interview. The manager doesn't want to muddy the waters by raising issues unrelated to the employee's KPIs. Also, the employee knows that nonjob performance isn't a factor in assessing their remuneration level, at least not openly. They understandably, aren't likely to raise their nonjob performance in the interview either. So, nonjob performance isn't used by the employee support their argument for a pay rise.

Not factoring in nonjob contributions, however, means an evaluation of performance is incomplete. Performing certain nonjob roles (such as those mentioned earlier) makes a significant difference. Even though these attributes can't be quantified, they affect personal and interpersonal performance. They are no less relevant, even if nonjob contributions are difficult to measure.

These nonjob factors can still be expressed qualitatively as KPIs. If you're interested in identifying KPIs for nonjob roles, look at my book, *The End of the Job Description: Shifting From a Job-Focus to a Performance-Focus* (Baker 2015).[2] I argue strongly in the book that nonjob roles should be considered in pay decisions.

For example, an employee who performs their nonjob roles can

- Elevate morale
- Build better teams
- Create harmonious working relationships
- Upgrade and improve systems and processes
- Apply new skills for the benefit and betterment of their work unit

Performing nonjob roles involve independent judgment, initiative, and enterprise. However, an overreliance on the job specification to make remuneration decisions devalues these contributions.

## Promoting and Planning Succession

Succession planning is the practice of identifying and developing people with the potential to fill key leadership positions in the future. Once more, the job description has too much sway in the succession planning process. Put simply: Plugging a gap in the org chart is usually decided on technical competence. Nontechnical qualities are generally overlooked.

The standard practice of succession planning is to groom someone with a similar technical skill set to the incumbent. What's more, the replacement is usually selected from the same functional area and the next level down in the organizational hierarchy. This appears a sensible practice, but it's not.

To prepare the successor for the eventual promotion, their training needs are analyzed based mostly on the technical requirements of the successive job. Although technical competence must be considered, nontechnical deficiencies are frequently neglected. The successor's training and development plan is predominantly job related, in other words. At best, development opportunities outside the scope of the job description are given lesser priority.

For instance, the successive position may involve extensive informal contact with several *difficult* stakeholders. This will be probably not be cited in the position's job specification. Joanna has been groomed to replace Mary as the senior finance officer, for example. As an internal service provider, Mary currently deals with many people on a variety of financial matters. Dealing effectively with people in other departments is crucial for success in Mary's role. But this vital feature of the role isn't covered in Joanna's training plan. Although Joanna's succession training emphasizes the technical aspects of Mary's role, success in her new role is largely dependent on building constructive working relationships with many people across the organization. Not including this nontechnical aspect in Joanna succession plan means she is ill prepared for the role.

Succession planning for leadership roles is often poorly done. Making the transition from a technical to a leadership role involves a fundamentally different skill set. The two roles are poles apart. For starters, the technical role is task related, and the leadership role is people related. The technical position involves doing the work, which entails a command of procedural knowledge, whereas the leadership position is overseeing the technical work done by others. A leader needs to motivate, communicate, influence, delegate, and coordinate. Why then do we promote people to leadership posts primarily on their technical know-how? The answer: Dependency on the task-specific job description to make promotional decisions.

It's nonsensical to promote people to leadership roles because they have great technical qualifications and skills. There are Dilbert-style jokes about this practice. Just because someone is a terrific engineer, for example, doesn't necessarily mean they will be a terrific leader of engineers. The skill sets aren't transferrable. A leader's knowledge of the intimate details of technical tasks—although undoubtedly useful—is less relevant than their ability to lead people to do the tasks. This all-too-familiar practice of promoting skilled technicians to managerial roles is another reason to rethink job design and performance.

This isn't only a problem for internal promotions. When recruiting externally to fill a leadership role, the selection decision is still based mainly on technical competence and experience. The first step in the selection process—even for roles that predominantly involve managing and leading—is to find candidates who match the functional criterion. If a candidate ticks all the technical boxes, the assumption is that they have what it takes to lead others in that discipline. With too much emphasis on technical knowledge and experience, succession planning and promotion is obstructed by the way we currently design and document jobs.

## Appraising and Reviewing

Managers conducting the annual performance review limit their appraisal to the contents of the employee's job description. The focus of the appraisal, in other words, is assessing the jobholder against the obligations of the job specification. This is considered conventional practice.

At the risk of being repetitive, this is another phase of the employee lifecycle that's too job centric.

The cost of sticking stringently to the letter of the job description at appraisal time is neglecting to review nonjob contributions. Employees— even when it's not warranted—get fair, or even good, evaluation ratings in review of their performance. Why does this happen? There are several reasons. But one explanation for unmerited ratings is the lack of attention on the appraisee's personal and interpersonal behavior. Many *average* or *above average* ratings are given to employees who demonstrate substandard, or even appalling, nonjob behavior.

---

### Where the Rubber Meets the Road

#### Sam's Awkward Appraisal

Sam is difficult to work with. Everyone dislikes Sam and refuses to deal with him unless they must. But he's a technically proficient IT professional. And so, he passes his appraisal in flying colors. John, Sam's manager, assesses his technical KPIs in the appraisal, as required by HR. He is reluctant to raise the elephant in the room: Sam's poor interpersonal dealings with his colleagues.

Here's a typical illustration of what I mean: Marcia is reluctant to develop her knowledge and skills. She's stopped growing and learning and refuses to up-skill, multiskill, or develop any new skill! Simon, her boss, gives Marcia a satisfactory rating, ignoring her learning deficiency. Following the performance review criteria, there's no scope for Simon to rate Marcia's capacity to continually learn and develop. He therefore feels reluctant to raise this matter with her, despite it being problematic. This trait is omitted, and so Marcia's poor attitude to learning is tacitly reinforced at appraisal time. There is a disparity between the appraisal outcome and reality.

The outcome of Maria's appraisal is that there's no compulsion for her to change their ways. Sidestepping these nonproductive behaviors, such as those displayed by Marcia, can be calamitous. Apart from the offender, this errant conduct adversely affects her colleagues and manager. It can negatively impact everyone directly or indirectly. By ignoring Marcia's poor attitude to learning new skills, it implies that this behavior is acceptable.

Performing at work—as I've pointed out continually—is more than accomplishing the KPIs in the job description.

This working document forms the backbone for all HR practices, six of which I've covered. Job specification—the dominant job design approach—originates from the century-old scientific management movement. The pervasiveness of the job description devalues nonjob behavior. Yet, it's apparent to most that the nonjob dimension of work has a substantial bearing on performance.

In summary, at the heart of the job description are several KRAs that together form the basis for job success. A new employee is selected on these KRAs. They are inducted into the organization with a mandate to achieve these KRAs. The employee is supported with job-related training programs. Having demonstrated their mastery of the job tasks, the employee is given several pay rises. With their technical nous, they're potentially promoted into a leadership position. The employee is selected, rewarded, promoted, and appraised on their task competency.

Even sacking someone is often justified based on poor job performance. The working document is used to provide convenient legal cover when someone is dismissed for nonjob-related reasons. But it's often dreadful nonjob behavior that's the real reason for firing someone. Nonetheless, it's the job description that's used to justify the dismissal. From entry to exit, the job description is ubiquitous in the life of an employee.

Successfully executing a bundle of tasks—we refer to as a *job*—will continue to be critical to success in the workplace. But there's more to employment success. Giving greater attention to the nonjob dimension of work—apart from job performance—is the key to elevating total performance at work. By stressing both job and nonjob dimensions, an organization shifts the accent from a job focus to a performance focus.

An overreliance on the job description can be nullified by applying the proactive framework we covered in Part I. Using the framework elevates the status of the nonjob dimension of performance.

In the next chapter, I revisit the four nonjob roles and how they can be used to empower employees.

## Top 10 Points

1. The three HR practices for rewarding people are remunerating and rewarding, promoting and planning succession, and appraising and reviewing.
2. Managers rely heavily on the job description to inform their decisions on pay rises.
3. Not factoring in nonjob contributions mean an evaluation of performance is incomplete.
4. Succession planning is the practice of identifying and developing people with the potential to fill key leadership positions in the future.
5. To prepare the successor for the eventual promotion, their training needs are analyzed based mostly on the technical requirements of the job.
6. It's nonsensical to promote people to leadership roles because they have great technical qualifications and skills.
7. Managers conducting the annual performance review limit their appraisal to the contents of the employee's job description.
8. The cost of sticking stringently to the letter of the job description at appraisal time is neglecting to review nonjob contributions.
9. This working document forms the backbone for all HR practices.
10. Even sacking someone is often justified based on poor job performance.

# CHAPTER 14

# Using the Proactive Framework to Promote Nonjob Performance

*A jobholder prepared (and encouraged) to perform these nonjob roles—in addition to completely satisfying the requirements of their job role— is accomplishing more than what's stated in their job description.*

In the last two chapters, I explained the way the job description obstructs enterprising behavior. I introduced the concept of the nonjob role and its significance to performing in the changing workplace. It's the nonjob role that I want to discuss here in this chapter. What are the key nonjob roles? Why are they important? And how can the proactive framework be applied to performance? These are the questions we explore.

Work is two dimensional. The job description details one dimension: the job. Nonjob work is the other dimension. As I've stated earlier, nonjob roles aren't covered equally, if at all, in the working document. In *The End of the Job Description*—I argue that by giving more attention to the nonjob dimension, the emphasis shifts from a job focus to a performance focus (Baker 2015).[1]

In summary, a performance focus—as distinct from a job focus—features four nonjob roles with the job role.

Accomplishing these four nonjob roles can significantly impact performance. More specifically, maintaining a positive attitude, being a team player, upgrading one's skills, and contributing to a more efficient and effective workplace can make a big difference. But these attributes play second fiddle to the job role.

Despite not featuring in the job description, the collaborative leader expects these roles to be performed by team members. Being enterprising and enthusiastic, working well in teams, continually growing, and contributing to a better work setting are reasonable expectations, after all.

Yet as I illustrated in the previous two chapters, the manager is pressured into paying most of their attention to the job dimension. The nonjob dimension is pushed into the background. But with more concentration, rather than a tacit expectation of performing these nonjob roles, a leader can drastically elevate their execution.

For example, think of the performance boost from:

- Morale-lifting behavior by showing positivity in adversity
- Sacrificing self-interest for the sake of the team's success
- Learning and applying a new skill on the job
- Coming up with a new and better way of doing something that benefits the business

But I'm sure you'd agree with me: these attributes are not common practices in most workplaces.

Everyone benefits from these traits. With a greater emphasis on the nonjob dimension, a leader will generate more empowerment from team members. The team member who fulfills positive nonjob behaviors adds value and enhances their employability. The customer and end user get more responsive service and better products. And shareholders and business owners own a more profitable company.

Although job design constrains work contributions to a clearly defined set of tasks and activities, people are capable, and most are willing to do more. And managers want employees to add value over and above their job role. Surveys show that managers value positive nonjob behaviors, apart from technical skill and experience. For ambitious employees in the right work setting—being proactive outside the scope of their job description—raises their career prospects.

In the past, in more stable and predictable times, the employees who followed the literal requirements of their job description were highly regarded. They were considered reliable and conscientious. Now, working in a changeable and unpredictable environment, the collaborative leader wants the team member to be enterprising when the situation calls for it. In this context, being enterprising is exhibiting proactive, positive behavior over and above the scope of the job description. For example, this includes

- Making practical suggestions for workplace improvements
- Being a positive and enthusiastic organizational citizen
- Displaying initiative to delight a customer with prudent but extraordinary customer service

Even though they aren't usually mentioned in the job description, they're nonetheless, valuable contributions.

To support my claim, consider the question: *What are the attributes that employer's value most in employees?* A list of the 10 most valued job attributes has been compiled from over 40 studies of medium- and large-scale employers, primarily in the United States, but also in other countries such as Australia, France, Singapore, and the United Kingdom. The top 10 characteristics identified in order of importance are as follows:

1. Enthusiasm and a positive attitude
2. Good communication skills
3. Self-motivated and initiative
4. Honesty
5. Good people skills
6. Showing persistence
7. Ability to work in a team
8. Organized and with a capacity to work under pressure
9. A willingness to learn and grow
10. Dependable and hardworking (Warner 2012)[2]

All 10 attributes are nonjob roles: they're undeniably valuable in any employment context. These 10 attributes apply in professional, semi-professional, and nonprofessional vocations; blue collar or white collar; indoor or outdoor; office based and remote, and traditional or nontraditional industries. When hiring, these are the attributes employers want, apart from technical qualifications and experience. But unfortunately, as stated, these nonjob behaviors aren't explicitly and consistently recognized and rewarded.

Figure 14.1 illustrates a more complete framework of work performance.

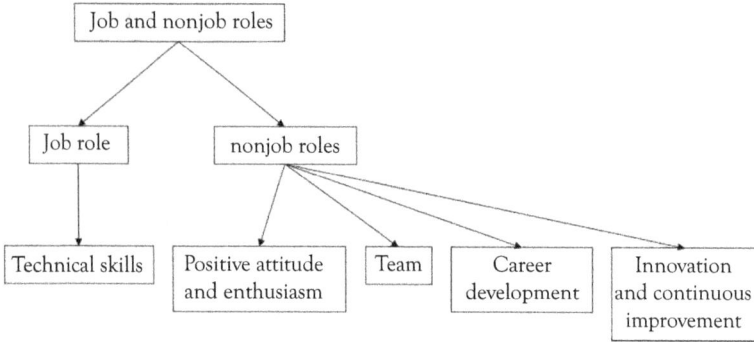

*Figure 14.1 Two-dimensional performance framework*

You can see from the illustration that there are two dimensions to work performance: job and nonjob. The job dimension is covered in the job specification and its appendage, the job description. The nonjob dimension includes four additional roles. There is myriad nonjob roles an employee can perform at work. But I have identified four universally important nonjob roles that effect performance.

The number of potential roles people can take on at work is limitless. Some roles are deliberately performed, while others are unconsciously carried out. Some are relevant, some not. Some take a split second to execute, some are ongoing. Some are appreciated, some not. Some are rewarded, some not. But a key question is this: Which nonjob roles are relevant in all organizations?

I want to define these four nonjob roles and explain their relevance. Furthermore, I want to show how the proactive framework can be used to promote more opportunities for the team member to exercise them.

So, let's explore these four nonjob roles in more depth.

Two of the nonjob roles in the framework can be categorized as *interpersonal* and the other two, *personal*.

## Positive Attitude and Enthusiasm Role

We begin with the *positive attitude and enthusiasm role*. It's impossible to be positive and enthusiastic all the time at work, or anywhere else for that matter. But equally, being negative and lacking enthusiasm, all the time, is impossible—and undesirable—too. However, I've met some people that test this claim! I'm sure you'd agree that people's attitude does affect those around them. And that's the main reason I have categorized this role as interpersonal, although it must be said that one's attitude is a personal choice.

I don't think it's unreasonable to expect people at work to maintain— most of the time—a positive attitude and enthusiasm. It's, after all, the number one job attribute listed earlier. With the pressure that comes with modern businesses constantly and rapidly chopping and changing—with relentless adjustments and disruptions—being positive builds and maintains morale.

Today, employees are now expected to do more with less; this adds another layer of pressure. Also, heightened competition, the increasing obsession with i-dotting and t-crossing, and the imposition of account-ability and transparency regimes elevate stress levels even further. Uphold-ing a positive attitude and being enthusiastic can be an antidote to these modern-day pressures and stresses. Cultivating a harmonious working environment is paramount and impossible to achieve with relentless neg-ativity. So, it's understandable—with all these present-day strains—why *enthusiasm and a positive attitude* are number 1 on the list of most wanted job attributes.

Here are three characteristics that support a positive attitude and enthusiasm at work:

- Being solution focused
- Displaying autonomy
- Contributing positive energy

*Being solution focused* means being prepared to find answers to prob-lems rather than complaining about them. *Displaying autonomy* refers to a willingness and capacity to work without close supervision. *Positive energy* is showing a positive and cooperative approach toward colleagues and the work that needs to be done. There are other characteristics of a positive attitude and enthusiasm. These three characteristics do, however, sum up the kind of proactive mindset that supports a positive attitude and enthusiasm.

Let's look at how the four proactive strategies (shared purpose, boundary management, information exchange, and proactive accountability) can be applied to foster the three characteristics of the nonjob role of positive attitude and enthusiasm.

Table 14.1 summarizes the relationship between the positive attitude and enthusiasm role and the proactive framework.

*Table 14.1  Positive attitude and enthusiasm role*

| Characteristics | Share purpose | Boundary management | Information exchange | Proactive accountability |
|---|---|---|---|---|
| Being solution focused | A shared purpose offers the employee clarity to find solutions to achieve the outcome | Boundary management gives the employee certainty on where they can (and can't) offer solutions | Exchanging information between the manager and employee encourages finding solutions | Proactive accountability confines employee solutions to areas where they're held accountable |
| Displaying autonomy | With a shared purpose, the employee feels confidence acting autonomously when needed | Boundary management identifies the areas where the employee is expected to think for themselves | By opening communication channels, the employee is urged to show initiative | Displaying autonomy is permissible in exceptional circumstances |
| Contributing positive energy | Shared purpose gives the employee the opportunity to work constructively with others | Clear boundaries provide the psychological safety to contribute positively | Encouraging an open exchange of ideas promotes positive energy | Proactive accountability doesn't necessarily promote positive energy |

As you can see, with the except of proactive accountability, three of the strategies are consistent with having a positive attitude and being enthusiastic.

# Team Role

The second interpersonal nonjob role in the framework is the *team role*. With the erosion of hierarchy and the corresponding flattening of organizational structures, teams are the dominant organizing work structure.

Being a team player is a sought-after attribute in the contemporary workplace. Employees are being called upon to participate in short- and long-term project teams, often with people they have never meet, let alone worked with before. These cross-functional project teams are set up to deal with specific problems or issues, utilizing people with a wide range of expertise and diversity of perspectives.

Working harmoniously and constructively with others in these team structures is vital. We saw that the seventh most valued job attribute is the *ability to work in a team*. Employers recognize the value and importance of teamwork.

Being a team player isn't as simple as it sounds, however. The team role is a complex combination of skills, knowledge, and attitude. For instance, to be successful working in a team, one need to

- Influence others and be open to being influenced by others
- Be accountable for their performance and be accountable for the team's performance
- Work cooperatively and harmoniously with others under duress, even when they don't want to
- Interact and exchange information with a variety of stakeholders beyond the team

Despite its contradictions, the ability to work in a team benefits colleagues, the leader, and the wider organization.

There are two proactive behaviors characteristic of being a team player. They are as follows:

- Leadership and influence
- Personal and team accountability

*Leadership and influence* in this context—apart from being open to being influenced—is the ability to persuade others in a positive way. *Personal and team accountability* refers to juggling personal performance with team performance. There are, of course, other behaviors that demonstrate being a good team player. However, these two characteristics require independent judgment.

Table 14.2 illustrates how the four proactive strategies influence the team role.

*Table 14.2  Team role*

| Characteristics | Share purpose | Boundary management | Information exchange | Proactive accountability |
|---|---|---|---|---|
| Leadership and influence | With a clear purpose, the team member is more likely use influence, when necessary, to achieve a common goal | Boundary management gives the team member guidance when it's suitable to assert their ideas | Freely exchanging information with the leader encourages the team member to speak up at the right time | In certain situations, the team member can take the lead, provided they're willing to be accountable for their actions |
| Personal and team accountability | A shared team purpose makes it apparent what is required | Boundary management clarifies expectations and accountabilities | Exchanging information fosters a collective team accountability | Proactive accountability makes it clear that the team member is accountable for their actions |

As you can see, all four strategies encourage mutual influence and balancing personal and team responsibilities.

Turning now to the two personal nonjob roles, starting with career development.

## Career Development Role

The *career development role* involves committing to continually growing and developing technically and personally. In other words, that means being a lifelong learner. We've all experienced people who have stopped growing and developing in their career. When the stagnant employee is challenged, they use lame excuses, like: "I'm too old to learn." Or, when invited to expand their career skills set, they respond with: "I'm just happy doing what I have always done." Having a desire to continually improve, upgrade, and expand one's skill-base and develop personally benefits them and their current and future employer.

Referring to the list, the ninth most valuable job attribute is *a willingness to learn and grow*. To develop oneself, involves an open-mindedness to new ways of doing things and a readiness to accept constructive feedback.

There are two core characteristics supporting the career development role:

- Technical development
- Personal development

The first characteristic relates to enhancing technical capability. *Technical development* involves training and retraining to master job skills. The second characteristic is developing oneself. *Personal development* can indirectly benefit work. Personal development covers time and stress management and interpersonal skills, for example.

Table 14.3 shows how the four strategies promote career development.

**Table 14.3** *Career development role*

| Characteristics | Share purpose | Boundary management | Information exchange | Proactive accountability |
|---|---|---|---|---|
| Technical development | With a shared purpose, the employee has a better understanding of their technical deficiencies | A greater awareness of the boundaries for independent judgment gives the employee an opportunity to identify technical training needs | Exchanging information between the manager and employee encourages feedback for job improvement | Organizations with a strong focus on proactive accountability value technical competence |
| Personal development | The employee working in a team with a shared purpose has a greater awareness of their personal strengths and opportunities for growth | Boundary management illuminates where the employee needs to develop personally | Information exchange helps the employee to openly discuss their personal development needs | Self-development benefits an individual when they use independent judgment for which they're ultimately accountable |

As you can see, the four strategies cultivate the personal and technical growth.

## Innovation and Continuous Improvement Role

The final nonjob (second personal) role in the framework is the *innovation and continuous improvement role*. While the career development role is concerned with improving the individual, the innovation and continuous improvement role is focused on improving the work setting.

Specifically, the innovation and continuous improvement emphasizes making constructive suggestions and changes in a workplace setting. The role covers a wide range of enhancement opportunities. For instance, it can include the following:

- Improving products or services
- Reducing time and cost
- Increasing output
- Improving safety
- Meeting deadlines
- Enhancing interpersonal cooperation
- Streamlining systems and processes

For a business to be viable in an increasingly competitive marketplace, it needs to be in a continual state of growth and development. Referring to the list, the attribute most closely aligned with this nonjob role is third on the list: *Self-motivated and initiative*. Employees have a role to play in continuous improvement. Generating new ideas and methods and thinking and acting without being prompted contribute to workplace development. Self-motivated and proactive employees drive progress.

But as I said in Chapter 12, getting people engaged in workplace improvement has, however, been a perennial and frustrating challenge since Peter Senge introduced us to the concept of the *learning organization* over a quarter of a century ago. This is a hangover from the old belief that it's the manager who should be the sole initiator of change in the business. What's more, modernizing and developing the workplace wasn't (and in some cases, still isn't) considered the employee's responsibility. But in the collaborative relationship (illustrated in Chapter 3), business improvement is a shared responsibility.

Two characteristics that support the innovation and continuous improvement role are as follows:

- Problem-solving and critical thinking
- Customer responsiveness

*Problem-solving and critical thinking* capabilities identify, define, critically analyze, and resolve work problems. This characteristic involves investigating and testing alternative ideas and approaches. Problem-solving and critical thinking capability equip people to look for and find better solutions to workplace dilemmas. *Customer responsiveness* is defined as identifying, understanding, building relationships with, and adapt to the needs of customers. All changes in the business should be mindful of its direct and indirect effect on the end user.

Table 14.4 summarizes the relationship between the four proactive strategies and the nonjob role of innovation and continuous improvement.

The innovation and continuous improvement role is valued in the first three strategies, but not so much with proactive accountability.

*Table 14.4 Innovation and continuous improvement role*

| Characteristics | Share purpose | Boundary management | Information exchange | Proactive accountability |
|---|---|---|---|---|
| Problem-solving and critical thinking | When the employee has a clear shared purpose, it helps them identify and solve problems | An awareness of the boundaries for independent judgment gives the employee a focus on where they have scope to act (and not act) | By exchanging information with their manager, the employee can discuss problems and solutions | It's only in extraordinary circumstances that the employee can show initiative and this requires critical thinking |
| Customer responsiveness | With a shared purpose, an employee has more freedom to exercise initiative to deal with their customers and end users | Boundary management clarifies the areas where the employee can be flexible with customers and end users | With a similar perspective as their manager, the employee can deal with customers and end users autonomously | With proactive accountability, the employee is constrained in the way they deal with customers and end users |

One can't argue with the relevance these four nonjob roles and how they can contribute to higher performance. The two-dimensional performance framework addresses the inherent weakness in conventional job design. This framework being two dimensional accounts for four nonjob roles the employee can play to better themselves and the business. These nonjob roles fill a gap in measuring performance that relies almost wholly on the job specification.

A jobholder prepared (and encouraged) to perform these nonjob roles—in addition to completely satisfying the requirements of their job role—is accomplishing more than what's stated in their job description. By taking on these nonjob roles, the employee is adding value to their employment and themselves.

As the research confirms, these (and other) nonjob roles are in high demand by employers. Promoting nonjob performance benefits employees and their careers and contributes to stronger business performance. From the employee's perspective, they are better served viewing their skills set and work identity as transferable and independent of any one organizational position or setting. Being shackled psychologically to the specifications of a job isn't ultimately useful anymore (I'm not sure it ever was!) to the employee or manager. The attributes and skills of the employee are portable. And it's evident that managers want to recruit people who are not only qualified and experienced but also eager to contribute beyond the boundaries of the job specification.

In Chapter 15, we look at job crafting as another way to nurture independent judgment and enterprise.

# Top 10 Points

1. Work is two dimensional. The job description details one dimension: the job. Nonjob work is the other dimension.
2. With a greater emphasis on the nonjob dimension, a leader will generate more empowerment from team members.
3. Although job design constrains work contributions to a clearly defined set of tasks and activities, people are capable, and most are willing to do more.

4. The four nonjob roles in the two-dimensional performance framework are positive attitude, team, career development, and innovation and continuous improvement.

5. The positive attitude and enthusiasm role is an asset in boosting morale in modern businesses that are constantly and rapidly chopping and changing.

6. The team role is vital with the erosion of hierarchy and the corresponding flattening of organizational structures.

7. The career development role involves committing to continually growing and developing technically and personally.

8. The innovation and continuous improvement role emphasize making constructive suggestions and changes in a workplace setting.

9. The two-dimensional performance framework addresses the inherent weakness in conventional job design.

10. As the research confirms, these (and other) nonjob roles are in high demand by employers.

# CHAPTER 15

# Job Crafting as an Antidote to Traditional Job Design

During employment, we devote approximately half our waking hours during the work week on the job. Sadly, most people see this enormous chunk of time as a struggle, or at least, a bore, looking forward to the weekend.

> *Paul works in IT in customer support. He spends most of his time on a help line but had a passion for testing and improving new software. Through discussions with his manager, Paul joined a group that tested new applications before they were launched in the company. This took up about three hours every month.*
>
> *Whilst Paul's role didn't substantially change through job crafting, he was delighted that his skill and passion for analysis of new applications was being recognized.[1]*

Having considered nonjob roles and their value in the last chapter, let's now turn our attention to the concept of job crafting as an antidote to the limitations of job specification. Job crafting is modifying a job to make it more engaging and meaningful for the jobholder. Furthermore, job crafting is done by the employee. They attempt to make constructive changes to their job, either by how they think about their job or what they do in their job (Petrou, Demerouti, Peeters, Schaufeli, and Hetland 2012).[2] Three drivers for job crafting are to:

- Gain more control over work
- Engage more in the work
- Develop better connections with others at work

These motivations lead to reshaping one's job.

Amy Wrzesniewski, professor of organizational behavior at Yale University, is credited with the concept of job crafting. She and her colleagues studied hospital cleaners job crafting, employees in a manufacturing firm, women working in advocacy nonprofit organizations, and IT workers for the past 20 years. The idea has been slow to take hold. Job crafting is an employee-centered strategy—as distinct from the manager-centered strategies covered in Parts I and II.

During our lifetime, most of us spend about 40 years in the workforce, unless we're fortunate enough to win lotto or reap a sizable inheritance. During employment, we devote approximately half our waking hours during the work week on the job. Sadly, most people see this enormous chunk of time as a struggle, or at least, a bore, looking forward to the weekend. For it is on the weekend that these people can then indulge in *worthwhile* pursuits. That's a big slab of potentially wasted time!

This raises several questions for me:

- What if most people thought their job was meaningful, or at least less mundane?
- What if people viewed their job as worthwhile?
- What difference would this make to people, organizations, and society overall?

Perhaps, job crafting can go some way to addressing these questions.

Instead of job design, what about job redesign? Job crafting involves taking proactive steps and applying practical actions to redesign the job. Job redesign can be done by either changing the tasks, altering relationships, or generating fresh perceptions of the work we are assigned (Berg, Dutton, and Wrzesniewski 2007).[3]

The assumption supporting job crafting is that by changing what we do and the rationale for doing it, the jobholder increases the meaning from their work. By redesigning the job, we are given, the jobholder can potentially gain more job satisfaction and the business can possibly be more productive.

With job crafting, there's still a need to do the core functional tasks that are part of the jobholder's responsibility, expressed in their job description. However, this is balanced by expressing the occupant's strengths and interests (Wrzesniewski, Berg, and Dutton 2010).[4] There's some evidence that job crafting improves work performance (Caldwell and O'Reilly 1990),[5] boosts motivation, and lifts engagement (Halbesleben 2010; Dubbelt, Demerouti, and Rispens 2019).[6] Job crafting can unleash the enterprising qualities of the individual. This is a promising and refreshing departure from the imposed shackles of job specification.

Let's briefly understand the three ways open for a jobholder to job craft.

The most obvious approach, referred to as *task crafting*, involves adding or eliminating certain activities, modifying the time or amount of effort spent on various job duties, or redesigning aspects of a given task. The second method, referred to as *relational crafting*, includes creating, maintaining, modifying, or eliminating relationships with others at work. And the third approach, called *cognitive crafting*, entails reframing the perception and interpretation of the job's purpose. We consider these in more detail, using illustrations.

## Task Crafting

Task crafting is adjusting the ways certain tasks are performed or taking on more or fewer tasks. Of the three forms of job crafting, task crafting is the most tangible approach, as indicated. Because it impacts the job specification directly, it's the most noticeable type of job crafting. The other two approaches indirectly effect the job.

With task crafting, the jobholder is essentially shaping or molding their work role to accommodate their strengths by adjusting the tasks they do, or not do. In practice, this can mean adding, dropping, or modifying the KRAs in the job description. The job tasks are redesigned to better suit the person in the role, in other words.

Consider two simple illustrations of task crafting.

Adele is a receptionist in an international hotel. She enjoys interacting with customers most of all. Adele takes it upon herself to call newly arrived guests, once they have settled into their room, and ask them if they have any questions that they can assist them with that they may have thought of while traveling up the elevator and unpacking. Apart from exhibiting superior customer service by initiating this room call, Adele has changed her view of her job as more then checking people into a hotel room. She considers herself as a source of information for a new guest in foreign city.

Not only is this an example of task crafting, but it's also motivated by cognitive crafting, or seeing her role differently.

As the second illustration, Harry, a bus driver, decides to give helpful sightseeing advice while traveling his regular route from the airport to the city. He's mindful that many of his passengers are from out of town. Harry perceives his job as more than driving a bus (cognitive crafting). By using his extensive local knowledge, Harry decides to use his extroverted personality to good effect. He decides to add sightseeing to his primary task of driving a bus.

In both illustrations, the jobholder decided to take on an additional task beyond their original job specification. Adele and Harry added these tasks because they were activities they enjoyed doing. But they were augmented because they saw their job as more than a receptionist and bus driver (cognitive crafting).

Adding tasks is one way to task craft, but there are other ways too. Task crafting can include changing the nature of certain responsibilities or taking away tasks. It might also involve dedicating a different proportion of time to certain tasks or devoting time to certain projects. These changes needn't affect the main focus of job the occupant is hired to do.

## Relational Crafting

Relational crafting focuses on changing the jobholder's interactions with others in carrying out their work. These working relationships, either within or beyond the workplace, are formed or reframed to be more effective on the job. This type of crafting emphasizes how people can restructure the way they deal with others to achieve their KPIs, in other words. Relational crafting can entail changing *who* the jobholder works with on different tasks and projects or *how* they communicate and engage stakeholders. For example, the employee can relationally craft by interacting with different departments they have neglected previously (who). Or they can make certain projects collaborative exercises that were attempted autonomously in the past (how).

Tom is a salesperson who sells digital solutions. He seeks out Marco, the firm's app designer in another department, to discuss making the user interface simpler for his customers. Although not a stakeholder, Tom's several interactions with Marco are fruitful and leads a more accessible menu that improves the company's product. With his understanding of his customer's needs, particularly their limited digital literacy, Tom shares his firsthand knowledge with Marco to improve the menu interface.

Here's another illustration of relational crafting: Marilyn is an architect who specializes in designing offices for large companies. She goes out of her way to organize several informal meetings with her clients on a new office design project. During these meetings, Marilyn—instead of looking at the current office layout—observes the way people are working and how they interact with one another. After several visits, Marilyn changes the office designs based on her observations and interactions with the customer.

In both cases, the employee preemptively seeks out others and this leads to changing their perspective and others to produce a better solution for the customer.

## Cognitive Crafting

Cognitive crafting is changing the way the jobholder thinks about their work. Furthermore, this approach refashioning the way one thinks about their job's impact on others. While the first two approaches to job crafting change the actions people take, this method involves choosing to reframe their mindset about what they do at work. With a change of perspective on the purpose of their job, the jobholder can find or create more meaning. Without a sense of purpose, work is often dull and unfulfilling.

Olivia is a room cleaner. Changing hotel bedsheets can easily be considered a mundane task. But Olivia doesn't see it that way. She views changing bedsheets as less about a dull cleaning task and more about making travelers' journeys more comfortable and memorable. Same task, different mindset.

Here is another illustration of cognitive crafting: Jon is a policy officer in a government agency. Policy officers are responsible for churning out endless policy papers. Jon doesn't think of it that way. He chooses to view this work as a valuable contribution to building a better society. Jon feels that the work he does can guide and inform good public policy for the benefit of his country.

An employee adopting this type of crafting thinks constructively about their job and how it contributes to a greater purpose beyond merely churning out the work.

---

## Where the Rubber Meets the Road

### *A Greater Sense of Meaning in her Job*

Candice Walker is a housekeeper at a university hospital. Her primary interest has always been the patients the organization serves and their families. From the time she started her job, she saw her work as much more than her cleaning responsibilities. Instead, she cognitively re-framed her work as a form of healing, playing a key role "in the house of hope." Defining her role as healer meant she paid additional attention to the tasks that might help people recover and leave the hospital more quickly. This meant dedicating extra care to cleaning bathroom features during the winter season, so her patients weren't endangered. It also meant anticipating and providing materials that might be in short supply so that the patient could feel "things were in control" and that they were moving toward a faster release to home. She also formed relationships with patients and their families, getting to know them as people, not just temporary patients.

Candice used her emotional intelligence to make gentle inquiries that showed care and interest, without overstepping boundaries. She used similar skills to discern who might need additional attention and conversation on a particular day or night because they were experiencing pain, fear, or loneliness. She would then alter which patients she spent time with so that her work could make a bigger difference in their lives. By cognitively crafting her job in these ways, Candice reported finding a greater sense of meaning in her job (Dutton and Wrzesniewski 2020).[7]

Job crafting—whether it's task, relational, or cognitive—requires positive proactive behavior from the employee; this can enable more meaning from work. Although job crafting is employee initiated, managers need to support it. With management encouragement, positive changes become an effective and sustainable form of enterprising behavior. The three types of job crafting—with their different emphases—are not mutually exclusive, however. Job crafters may exercise any combination of the three dimensions.

Using any of the three approaches, or a combination, the employee can redesign their work to capitalize on their strengths and interests. The employee, in other words, with the support of their manager, can change their job to be more meaningful and productive. To be clear: Job crafting is not completely abandoning important tasks and doing whatever comes to mind.

In the next chapter, we will consider some of the key considerations for applying job crafting and how that can be implemented successfully.

# Top 10 Points

1. Job crafting is modifying a job to make it more engaging and meaningful for the jobholder.
2. Job crafting is an employee-centered strategy—as distinct from the manager-centered strategies covered in Parts I and II.
3. Job crafting involves taking proactive steps and applying practical actions to redesign the job.
4. The assumption supporting job crafting is that by changing what we do and the rationale for doing it, the jobholder increases the meaning from their work.
5. There are three types of job crafting: task crafting, relational crafting, and cognitive crafting.
6. Task crafting is adjusting the ways certain tasks are performed or taking on more or fewer tasks.
7. Relational crafting focuses on changing the jobholder's interactions with others in carrying out their work.

8. Cognitive crafting is changing the way the jobholder thinks about their work.
9. Job crafting—whether it's task, relational, or cognitive—requires positive proactive behavior from the employee; this can enable more meaning from work.
10. Using any of the three approaches, or a combination, the employee can redesign their work to capitalize on their strengths and interests.

# CHAPTER 16

# The Application of Job Crafting

*… the proactive framework assists in facilitating the
right conditions for job crafting to flourish.*

In this final chapter of Part III, I want to discuss some of the important issues associated with implementing job crafting in a work setting. Can job crafting coexist with job specification? And if so, how? While job specification is a top-down, management-driven job design strategy, job crafting is an employee-driven activity. Job specification is designed by managers and job crafting is initiated by jobholders. On the surface, job crafting and job specification seem incompatible.

An employee engages in job crafting by reshaping the boundaries of their job in three possible ways:

- The tasks
- The relationships
- The mindset

Job crafting resists the idea of a jobholder being a passive recipient of a bundle of tasks and processes. Crafting integrates proactive changes to the job, whereas job specification is designed to be following. They can—and should—coexist, however.

Before exploring how job crafting can be applied intentionally, we should acknowledge that the job one does is being modified over time, whether they're aware of it or not (Wrzesniewski and Dutton 2001).[1] People tend to accentuate the things they enjoy and reduce the parts they may find dull, often unconsciously. This is true about life in general and isn't confined to work; it's part of the human condition. Reshaping the job makes work more enjoyable—or at least, less mundane. It also contributes to a healthier work identity. Job crafting can occur naturally or purposefully.

Purposeful job crafting, however, is a valuable means of adapting what is done at work to changing demands in the marketplace. Asking for support from the manager and prioritizing one's workload are two typical, intentional ways to cope with an unexpected situation at work, for example. Although all jobholders craft to some extent, their place in the organizational pecking order can have a bearing on how it's done. Leaders will start job crafting and subsequently frame their team's expectations around those changes. Junior employees, on the other hand, tend to job craft after receiving approval from their manager. While everyone is generally primed to job craft, how it's done depends on hierarchical status.

Though job crafting is employee driven, the manager has a role to play, besides giving their approval. The manager can stimulate a conducive environment for the employee to initiate job crafting. While managers shouldn't instruct individuals on what or how to job crafted, they should create the right conditions for it to blossom.

As you know, I'm critical of conventional job design, particularly its limitations in dealing with the demands of a dynamic marketplace. Job specification—the genesis of job design—is inflexible and ill-equipped to be responsive to the dramatic changes in work in the past several decades. A one-size-fits-all framework has outlived its purpose. Job crafting can, however, enhance job design to address the challenges of a turbulent world we live and work in.

Let's now compare and contrast job specification and job crafting and how they can complement each other.

The fundamental distinction of the two methods is the instigator. Job specification is designed by management and imposed on the jobholder, whereas job crafting is initiated by the jobholder, with the support of management. Job specification is systemic, intended to make organizational work efficient and effective. The jobholder is expected to fit in with its design, without input. With job crafting, the responsibility for changing the job's parameters is left with the jobholder. Moreover, the jobholder must be the instigator for job crafting to work.

A second difference is the aim of both approaches. Job crafting's intends to enrich the jobholder, while the purpose of job specification is to optimize organizational performance. Yet, job specification, by design, stifles enterprise and dampens creativity—essential attributes in today's world of work. Furthermore, job specification renders work as procedural and therefore mundane. This deprives the jobholder of their autonomy.

Although distinct in origin and aim, the two approaches have similarities. Task crafting, one dimension of job crafting, is comparable to job specification. Both strategies emphasize the task-related functions in the job description. Task crafting and job specification consider the technical aspects of the job. They both assess adding, dropping, or modifying tasks in the job description. The other two dimensions of job crafting: relational and cognitive, bear no real similarities to job specification.

Since job crafting is initiated by the jobholder and job specification by the management, they can potentially work in tandem. By blending the top-down and bottom-up approach, redesigning a job through crafting can factor in the needs of the individual jobholder. Combining job design and job crafting can make improvements from a dual perspective.

For instance, job crafting leads to higher levels of employee engagement. Being engaged in work has a positive impact on job performance. The jobholder, through crafting, can boost their performance by being appropriately resourcefulness. When a manager supports intentional job crafting, it elevates employee empowerment.

For these reasons, job crafting should supplement—not replace—the top-down job design strategy. This blended approach, if applied effectively, will be an inducement for the business's top talent to stay longer and attractive quality applicants from other businesses.

Done well, job crafting adapts a generic job specification to better suit the strengths and preferences of the jobholder. While all employees will undoubtedly benefit from a job redesign, it's especially appealing to specific groups of employees. These groups include older employees, employees with disabilities or health problems, and parents with young children, particularly female employees. People in these categories are challenged more than others working within an inflexible job specification framework.

## Special Employment Needs

Older employees generally value work that provides meaning. In the twilight of their career, these employees want to feel useful, respected, and recognized. Also, older employees are inclined to prioritize personal relationships with colleagues, family, and friends. These relationships are often more important to them than work goals, which doesn't mean they're any less inclined to achieve business outcomes. With invaluable experience, these employees are a special group with specific needs. For instance, they have a wealth of work (and life) experience. They have accumulated a bank of tacit knowledge that can be shared with less experienced employees. Mentoring, for example—although not explicitly stated in their job description—is one way they can continue to make a valuable contribution. In the right circumstances, an older worker is typically happy to impart their knowledge and adapt their extensive skills set where necessary.

Research shows that job crafting benefits employees with health problems and disabilities (Srivastava and Chamberlain 2005).[2] Returning to work and job retention are top-of-mind for these employees. Reshaping their job can assist them in getting back to work and retain their employment. Scope to restructure their job gives these employees with special needs the opportunity to continue to make a worthy contribution.

Women and employees with young children are another category that needs particular attention. Parents of young children, especially mothers, have greater family demands than those with older children. Work and family roles are a constant juggling act. With this delicate balance—one that most parents have experienced—employees with young children can benefit from job crafting. Redesigning their work responsibilities helps immensely and gives them the flexibility to cope with the demands of family responsibilities.

Minorities and young employers are other groups that benefit from bottom-up adjustments to their job. People from marginal groups often have different life experiences and values; their distinctive perspective can be used to enrich the work environment. For instance, someone who hails from a country with a collectivist culture will probably see value in relational crafting that enhances cross-functional communication.

By resharing their job, they may strengthen neglected internal relationships. And employees in the early stages of their career lack awareness of their strengths and opportunities for growth. Adapting their jobs gives a new employee the chance to grow and develop, instead of floundering.

As I said, all employees can benefit from job crafting. But job crafting is a promising way to create a healthy and motivating work setting for groups who don't fit the mold of a generic job specification. What's more, employees have different needs at different life stages. Being more conscious of these various stages, leaders can cater for these career phases.

## Designing a Job Crafting Program

I want to now turn to how to facilitate a job crafting program.

A job crafting program consists of four steps:

1. Training
2. Recording work activity
3. Reflecting
4. Planning

Each step builds upon the previous step.

Let's consider each stage briefly.

To begin, organize a job crafting workshop. This training is designed to educate employees on the concept of job crafting, how it works, and its benefits.

After the training session, participants complete a logbook to record their work activities. Employees record in 15-minute intervals the work they do over the course of week. Why only a week? It's likely that a week will cover most, if not all, the activities an employee engages in.

During the reflection meeting, the team comes together and discusses their thoughts from their completed logbook. They discuss their successes, problems, and solutions throughout the previous week. Specifically, individuals are looking for aspects of their work that could be open to job crafting. They share their thoughts and ideas with colleagues, seeking feedback and ensuring that their proposed job changes won't adversely affect others in the team.

Based on the outcomes of the reflection meeting, team members identify one to three ideas for job crafting. The team member then discusses their plan with the team leader. A leader's role in this discussion is to explore ways they can best support their team members to successfully apply the changes.

This program is designed to inspire proactive job crafting behavior. Job crafting is an effective tool to embolden employees to adjust their work role to suit their strengths, preferences, and needs. Teams benefit too by collaborating more effectively; they become more malleable. Businesses profit in two ways: First, job crafting bolsters the top-down job design. Job specification is augmented by accommodating individual strengths, circumstances, and needs. Second, this dual job design approach gives the business a competitive advantage in retaining and attracting top talent. Jobs are more appealing since they're flexible to suit the needs of the incumbent or a prospective employee.

Job crafting works on two levels. At one level, the job is a better fit for the jobholder's preferences and needs. At another level, job crafting empowers the jobholder. In other words, it offers the individual a chance to shape their work role; the employee has more freedom and autonomy. At both levels, this method gives the jobholder a chance to maximize their strengths and minimize their weaknesses. Obstacles arise with the imposition of a one-size-fits-all job design. This inflexibility is often a source of frustration for both the jobholder and their manager.

Although employee initiated, we shouldn't underestimate the role of the leader. Their role is to support suitable job crafting initiatives. Again, I am not suggesting the top-down job design framework should be dismantled and replaced. What I am suggesting is that the leader should permit, motivate, and train team members to redesign their jobs in a way that better suits them to accomplish business goals. A leader's encouragement can strengthen—not weaken—the job design framework.

In addition to using the proactive framework to promote nonjob roles, job crafting is another useful way to maximizing performance through empowerment. Like exercising nonjob roles, job crafting is driven by the employee. These strategies enable the enterprising qualities of employees to prosper. Nonjob roles and job crafting reshape the working relationship between the jobholder and their work.

The proactive framework assists in facilitating the right conditions for job crafting to flourish. Shared purpose aligns the needs and interests of the organization and individual. This strategy stimulates enterprising behavior in the pursuit of a clear purpose. When employees have a sure purpose, it becomes apparent where they can job craft. Boundary management involves carefully communicating the kind of initiative desired and—at the same time—where initiative isn't warranted. These boundaries provide employees with guidelines for desirable job crafting behavior. Information exchange opens the communication channels between manager and employees to work collaboratively. Dialog naturally leads to discussing opportunities for job crafting and how the leader can support their team member to do so. Proactive accountability still permits initiative, but only at their own risk. This strategy isn't likely to increase job crafting activity. It's a useful strategy, however, to confine employee activity to the job specification, except in exceptional circumstances, such as a crisis. Nonetheless, the first three strategies of the proactive framework will be helpful to foster a positive environment for job crafting to occur.

This completed Part III. The focus of Part III was on the employee's relationship with their job. In Part IV, I discuss a useful process to provide feedback to a manager on the four strategies in the proactive framework. To what extent is the manager using or not using the strategies? This feedback is a good foundation for developing a plan-of-action to improve the manager's capacity to break the proactive paradox.

## Top 10 Points

1. Job crafting resists the idea of a jobholder being a passive recipient of a bundle of tasks and processes.
2. Job crafting can occur naturally or purposefully.
3. Job crafting can enhance job design to address the challenges of a turbulent world we live and work in.
4. All employees can benefit from job crafting. But job crafting is a promising way to create a healthy and motivating work setting for groups who don't fit the mold of a generic job specification.
5. A job crafting program consists of four steps.
6. Job crafting training educates employees on the concept.

7. After the training, participants complete a logbook to record their work activities.

8. The reflection meeting looks at aspects that could be open to job crafting.

9. The final step in the program is to design a job crafting plan.

10. This program is designed to inspire proactive job crafting behavior.

# PART IV

# Measuring Proactive Behavior

# CHAPTER 17

# Manager Profile and Action Plan

*By using the team profile and action plan, you'll get a thorough grasp of the extent that you are using the four proactive strategies to maximizing performance through empowerment.*

In this final chapter, I'll provide you with a practical step-by-step action-planning process to strengthen the work environment for proactive behavior to prosper in the right places. This process is based on the proactive framework we've discussed throughout the book. The focus is on the manager's leadership style, beginning with an assessment of their application of the four strategies. Often, the dilemma in any change initiative is knowing where to begin—it's no different with developing leadership capabilities.

The place to start is to establish a set of benchmarks, based on the proactive framework. These benchmarks answer the question: *What are the leader's strengths and opportunities for growth in terms of encouraging empowerment?*

By benchmarking the manager against the KPIs for each strategy, they can then develop an action plan to boost their leadership performance. With certainty on where to begin their development, the manager saves time and energy. They can then focus on applying certain actions based on the feedback. Changing certain leadership behaviors in one area can positively impact other areas in the report.

Should you require more support beyond these final pages, you are welcome to contact me.[1]

Figure 17.1 is an illustration of the steps in the action plan.

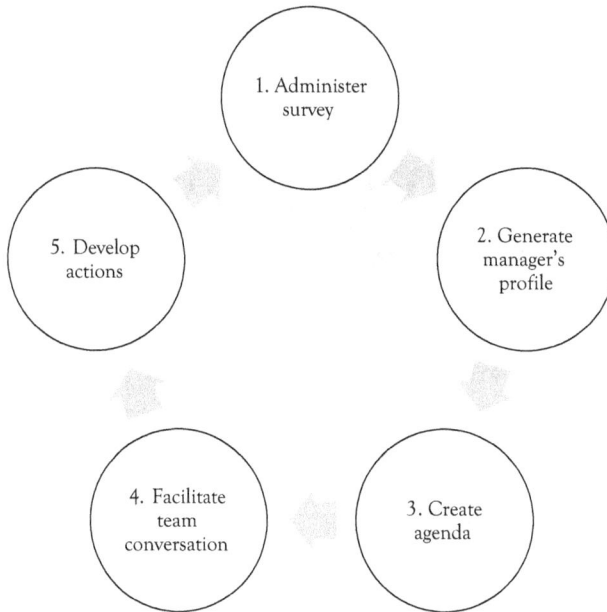

*Figure 17.1 Action plan*

The first thing you'll notice about the action plan is that it's cyclical rather than linear. Action planning in this case is an ongoing process that becomes part of the manager's development.

I'll now walk you through each of the five steps in Figure 17.1.

## Administer Survey

The first task is to establish the inputs for feedback. The aim is to gain a realistic picture of how the manager is performing. In the survey method, there are three perspectives to consider:

- Manager
- Manager's manager (boss)
- Team members

With three perspectives, the survey method is commonly referred to as a "360" or multirater. Multiple perspectives account for the view of the manager and those working closely with them. Using a multirater approach, a comparison can be made between the perspectives of the manager, their manager, and their team members. Surveying three perspectives is a more comprehensive approach than just surveying one perspective, such as the manager.

Selecting the first two inputs (manager and manager's manager) is straightforward. Choosing the team member input is usually straightforward too, if the team is clearly defined. However, if the team isn't clearly defined, then the best course-of-action is to select those people who report directly to the manager. Either way, I would aim for at least four team perspective inputs.

The profile is administered online, so permission will need to be obtained from all participants. With their approval, all participants are sent an invitation to complete the survey. The survey should take no more than 15 minutes to complete. Each participant is issued with a unique key to protect their anonymity. This means team member responses can't be attributable to the individual. The manager and their manager's responses, however—being one-person perspectives—are obvious in the report.

## Generate Manager's Profile

Once everyone has completed the survey, a manager's profile report is generated. The report covers 40 statements (10 for each proactive strategy). Although randomized in the survey, the statements and their responses in the report are organized into four sections: shared purpose, boundary management, information exchange, and proactive accountability.

For each strategy, the 10 statements have been crafted around relevant KPIs covered in Part II.  Below is the structure and summary of the relevant KPIs.

*Shared purpose*

- A clarity of team purpose.
- A minimum of conflict around priorities.
- A lack of confusion with direction.
- A lack of secrecy and a surplus of transparency.
- A high level of truthfulness and honesty.

*Boundary management*

- Boundaries for displaying initiative are apparent.
- A collective understanding of the extent and limit of individual authority to make decisions.
- Minimal confusion around when to show independent judgment.
- A collective understanding of when not to act autonomously.
- Evidence of frequent dialog between the manager and team members.

*Information exchange*

- A high level of trust between the manager and team members.
- Evidence of information sharing opportunities.
- Some evidence of the manager being influenced by team members.
- Employees view themselves as partners rather than subordinates.
- Some decisions are made by consensus.

*Proactive accountability*

- A clear understanding of when independent judgment is prohibited.
- A clearly defined chain of command for decision making.
- Compliance is the overriding consideration over enterprise.
- Employees understand that they will be held accountable for using independent judgment.
- Procedures and processes are valued over enterprising behavior.

You can contact me for more information on the survey content.[2]

Participants have three options when answering the survey statements: *agree*, *disagree*, or neither agree nor disagree (*neither*). A *neither* response can be posted for several reasons. *Neither* could be an indication that an observable KPI isn't always consistent with the statement. Or it could mean that the respondent doesn't know or isn't entirely convinced to *agree* or *disagree* with a statement. It could also mean that there's scope for improvement.

Let's turn to one of the two graphics in the team profile report. The first graphic—summarizing each strategy—illustrates the extent of agreement and disagreement (congruence) for the 10 statements related to that strategy. The other graphic is a histogram showing the percentage of aggregate *agree* and *disagree* responses for the three perspectives. I'll elaborate on the first of these two graphical representations.

Figure 17.2 illustrates the seven possible outcomes for a response to a statement.

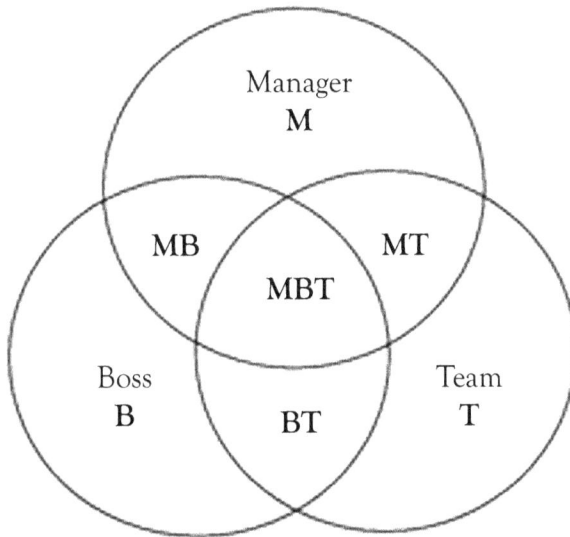

*Figure 17.2  Potential outcomes*

- **M** represents an aggregate view shared exclusively by the manager.
- **B** represents an aggregate view shared exclusively by the boss (manager's manager).
- **T** represents an aggregate view shared exclusively by the team.
- **MB** represents an aggregate view shared by the manager and boss, but not the team.

- **BT** represents an aggregate view shared by the boss and team, but not the manager.
- **MT** represents an aggregate view shared by the team and manager, but not the boss.
- **MBT** represents an aggregate view shared by all three perspectives.

The aggregate result, wherever it arises in the graphs in the manager's profile report, can be positive; that is, there's a majority view in one, two, or three perspectives that agreed with a statement. Furthermore, this result suggests a general perception that a KPI is evident. Or the opposite might be the case; that is, one or more of the three perspectives disagreed with a statement. This type of result indicates that an overall perception that a KPI is not apparent. An aggregate positive or negative result shared by all three perspectives (represented in the **MBT** space in the graphic) would indicate that there's overwhelming or underwhelming agreement or disagreement, respectively, for a statement in the survey. Results in the **MBT** space can suggest a positive or negative result in the manager's profile report.

The third possible response is a mixed or *polarized* response. These results indicate varied opinions about a statement, without a majority favoring either a positive or negative outcome. A *polarized* response can occur in all areas except **M** or **B**. Since **M** and **B** represent the exclusive view of the one perspective—the manager and boss—only three results are possible: agree, disagree, or neither. But in the other five areas on the graphic, where there is more than one input, a *polarized* result is possible. A *polarized* result means that there is an even split between *agree* and *disagree* responses for a statement in the survey.

A *polarized* result could show up in the team (**T**) perspective or between two perspectives (**MT**, **BT**, or **MB**). If the view within one or two perspectives is *polarized*, it's signified by the figure "0." *Polarized* responses, wherever they show up in the profile, can be interpreted in several ways and need to be discussed with the survey participants to understand their possible meaning.

The final type of result is *neither*. A *neither* response to a statement can be illustrated in the profile in one or more of the three perspectives (**M**, **B**, and **T**). This occurs when the aggregate response for manager, boss, and team is *neither* for a statement.

All seven possible aggregate results (**M**, **B**, **T**, **MB**, **BT**, **MT**, and **MBT**) can be significant. To illustrate, an aggregate *agree* or *disagree* result shared by all three perspectives (represented in **MBT** in Figure 17.2) is an indicator of an overwhelming perception that a KPI is either observable or imperceptible in the manager's behavior. For example, consider an aggregate *agree* result (represented as **MBT**) for the following two survey statements in the survey:

- I communicate a clear purpose to my team.
- My team has a clear purpose of their role.

Where all three perspectives *agree* with these two statements, this indicates a strong perception that the manager has effectively communicated a clear purpose to their team (a KPI for shared purpose). On the other hand, an aggregate *disagree* result (again in **MBT**) for both statements would point to an overwhelming opinion (including the manager) that he or she hasn't communicated a clear purpose to the team. While results recorded in **MBT** are definitive, other results recorded in the intersections between the three perspectives (**MB**, **BT**, and **MT**) are less so.

By discussing the results of the profile report with the team, the manager can gain a better understanding of the result. Questions such as

- Why is the manager positive about this KPI, when the team was not?
- What have team members observed that the manager has missed?

can be discussed to generate greater awareness. Asking these types of questions may clarify the profile's results and generate more insight.

The manager's profile report is a catalyst for a team conversation. Results in the report don't explain the reasons for similar or differing perceptions between and within the three perspectives. The report does provide a sound basis for developing an agenda for a constructive team discussion, however. We will discuss more about the team conversation shortly.

Figure 17.3 provides a real-life team example of the summary outcome for the strategy of boundary management.

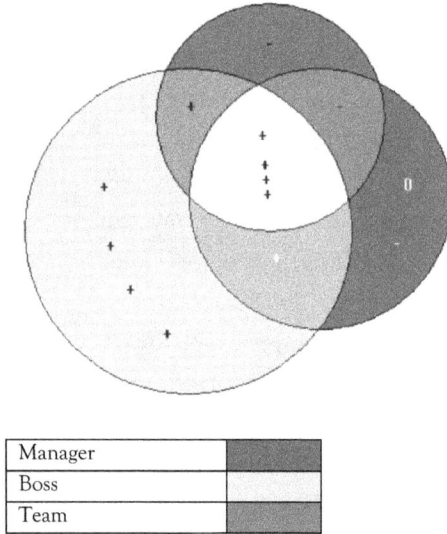

| Manager | |
| --- | --- |
| Boss | |
| Team | |

*Figure 17.3 Boundary management*

In Figure 17.3, a "+" symbol represents an aggregate positive result for 4 of 10 statements related to boundary management in the **MBT** space. Aggregate negative results are shown as a "–" symbol. You can see there are three in Figure 17.3 in the **M**, **MT**, and **T** spaces.

Note the three intersecting circles are different sizes. Each time an aggregate response to a statement is *neither* agree nor disagree, the radius of the circle reduces by 10 percent. The smaller a circle, the more aggregate *neither* responses from the participants representing that perspective.

Data in the report are represented statistically too. Table 17.1 shows an illustration of one statement from a manager profile.

Each of the 40 statements are represented statistically, like the one above. Survey participants can also make comments that are reflected in the report in a separate section.

In summary, the manager profile report is formatted into four sections based on the proactive framework. Within each section of the report, data

*Table 17.1  Statistical representation*

| Q.4 I am a good listener. | | |
|---|---|---|
| Perspective | Aggregate result | Breakdown |
| Manager | Agree | |
| Boss | Agree | |
| Stakeholders | Disagree | Agree: 20% (1/5)<br>Neither: 20% (1/5)<br>Disagree: 60% (3/5) |

for the four strategies are clearly presented. Each strategy is represented in summary like Figure 17.3 as well as in histogram format. Below these two graphics are the statistical results of the 10 statements related to that strategy, like Table 17.1. And at the end of the report are anonymous comments from participants.

## Create Agenda

The next step in the action-planning process is selecting one strategy from the profile report for a team discussion with their manager. The purpose here is to use the survey data to guide and inform a team conversation. Select the strategy with the most potential for improvement. Developing one strategy will improve other strategies. Specifically, enhancing one proactive strategy—with interdependencies between strategies—is likely to positively affect more independent judgment in other places.

Instead of being paralyzed with myriad options, focusing on one strategy at a time is a sound pathway. So, the agenda for discussion should be confined to one strategy and the 10 statements relating to that strategy in the profile report.

## Facilitate Team Conversation

To assist you to facilitate a constructive team conversation, here are some questions to start the team discussion:

- Do the results surprise you or not? Why? How?
- What are some examples to verify these findings?

- What can I do and what can you do to improve this strategy?
- What can I change and what can we as a team do to change?
- What can we do to continue the good outcomes of the report?

## Develop Actions

From the team discussion, the next step is to develop some practical and realistic actions. Use the tools and suggestions in Part II. For example, if it's evident in the post report discussion that people are not clear of the team's purpose, create a team purpose statement (see Chapter 9). This will help to minimize confusion in the future.

To monitor team progress, repeat the cycle, beginning with another team profile report. I recommend completing the survey annually. Steps 3, 4, and 5 in the action-planning process should be done at least once throughout the year between profile reports. If improvements are evident from the subsequent annual survey report, congratulations! You and your team are moving in the right direction. Commence a similar process with another strategy next year. Again, use the relevant practices for that strategy in Part II.

Besides shifting focus to another strategy to develop, the only other change that maybe necessary is adding or removing survey participants. It's preferable to invite the same participants to complete successive surveys for consistency. But in practice, it's likely, as time passes, that there will be changes in the team. Adjust for this by inviting new and removing redundant participants to offer their perspective.

By using the team profile and action plan, you'll get a thorough grasp of the extent that you are using the four proactive strategies to maximizing performance through empowerment. More specifically, it'll indicate to you where you can improve and where you are doing well. This process will improve your interactions with your team. As I've said throughout the book, using the proactive framework will build the type of climate conducive for team members to exhibit independent judgment in the right ways and in the right places. Developing collaborative leadership also makes it clearer where being proactive isn't appropriate. In short, you are breaking the proactive paradox.

I wish you well on your leadership journey.

## Top 10 Key Points

1. There are five steps in the action-planning process.
2. The first step is to administer the team profile survey.
3. The team profile survey uses a 360-degree methodology.
4. Step 2 is to generate the team profile report.
5. The team profile report consists of 40 statements, categorized into four sections, consistent with the four proactive strategies.
6. The third step is to create an agenda for a team discussion on the report.
7. The agenda should focus on one strategy.
8. Step 4 is to facilitate a team discussion.
9. The team discussion concentrates on one strategy with the potential for the most improvement.
10. The final step is to develop some practical and realistic actions.

### Thank you!

Thank you for joining me on the journey toward improving employee empowerment. I hope you have found *Breaking the Proactive Paradox: Maximizing Performance Through Empowerment* thought provoking and useful!

If you loved the book and have a moment to spare, we I would really appreciate a short review on the site where you purchased.

Your help in spreading the word is gratefully received!

## Need More Help?
### Manager Profile

If you wish to apply the manager's profile explained in the last chapter, please contact me direct at tim@winnersatwork.com.au, and we can arrange this for you. It is reasonably priced and is a great place to start in your continuing journey as a leader.

### Industry updates

If you would like to receive my monthly newsletter with interesting article and tools for leaders, please go to www.winnersatwork.com.au/latest-industry-updates/

### Speaking and Consulting

I speak regularly on this topic and others around the world. If you would like to engage me in your upcoming conference, contact me at tim@winnersatwork.com.au
I am also available for consulting work too.

### Useful Leadership Tools

Go to www.winnersatwork.com.au for some useful tools to assist you, your team, and organization.

### Other Books by Tim Baker

*The 8 Values of Highly Productive Companies: Creating Wealth From a New Employment Relationship*

*The End of the Performance Review: A New Approach to Appraising Employee Performance*

*Attracting and Retaining Talent: Becoming an Employer of Choice*

*The New Influencing Toolbox: Capabilities for Communicating With Influence*

*Conversations at Work: Promoting a Culture of Conversation in a Changing Workplace*

*The End of the Job Description: Changing From a Job-Focus to Performance-Focus*

*Performance Management for Agile Organizations: Overthrowing the Eight Management Myths That Hold Businesses Back*

*Bringing the Human Being Back to Work: The 10 Performance and Development Conversations Leaders Must Have*

*Winning Teams: The Eight Characteristics of High Performing Teams*

### Where You Can Find Me

LinkedIn: www.linkedin.com/in/winnersatwork/

Twitter: @winnersatwork

SlideShare: www.slideshare.net/DrTimBaker

Facebook: www.facebook.com/winnersatworkptyltd

Website: www.winnersatwork.com.au

Instagram: www.instagram.com/winnersatwork/

Pinterest: www.pinterest.com.au/tbaker1525/

YouTube: www.youtube.com/c/TimBakerthoughtleader

SlideShare: www.slideshare.net/DrTimBaker

# Notes

## Chapter 1

1. www.mindtools.com/pages/article/fostering-initiative-team.htm.
2. Campbell (2000).
3. Campbell (2000).
4. www.citrix.com/en-au/news/announcements/apr-2020/remote-work-the-new-normal.html
5. Pink (2011).

## Chapter 2

1. Baker (2014).
2. The Industrial Revolution was the transition from creating goods by hand to using machines. Its start and end are widely debated by scholars, but the period generally spanned from about 1760 to 1840.
3. It's become a trendy managerial acronym: VUCA, short for volatility, uncertainty, complexity, and ambiguity, and a catchall for "Hey, it's crazy out there!"
4. Jacobs (2020).

## Chapter 3

1. Baker (2014).
2. Baker (2009).
3. Baker (2014).
4. Middlemiss (2015).

## Chapter 4

1. Jones (2016).

# Chapter 6

1. Baker (2017).
2. Baker (2009).

# Chapter 7

1. Nayer (2014).
2. Kouzes and Posner (2011).
3. Kouzes and Posner (2011).
4. Kouzes and Posner (2011).
5. Baker and Warren (2015).
6. Maslow's hierarchy of needs is a theory of motivation which states that five categories of human needs dictate an individual's behavior.
7. Hsiao-Wen Ho, Ghauri, and Larimo (2018).
8. www.goodreads.com/quotes/118880-no-one-cares-how-much-you-know-until-they-know
9. Goffee and Jones (2000).
10. www.ccl.org/articles/leading-effectively-articles/closing-the-gap-between-intent-and-impact/

# Chapter 8

1. Senge (1999).
2. https://en.wikipedia.org/wiki/GROW_model#cite_note-1
3. https://en.wiktionary.org/wiki/give_a_man_a_fish_and_you_feed_him_for_a_day;_teach_a_man_to_fish_and_you_feed_him_for_a_lifetime

# Chapter 9

1. http://toolbox.hyperisland.com/team-purpose-culture
2. Baker (2021).
3. Baker (2015).
4. www.gitadaily.com/sutra-6-words-shape-worlds-watch-your-words/

# Chapter 10

1. Gardner and Matviak (2020).
2. Patterson, Grenny, Maxfield, and Switzler (2013).
3. www.brightlaw.com.au/draft-code-of-ethics-for-financial-advisers/
4. www.brightline.org/learning-from-crisis-mode/
5. Straw, Sandelands, and Dutton (1981).

# Chapter 11

1. De Smet, Hewes, and Weiss (2020).
2. Gallo (2011).
3. Baker (2015).
4. Castellano (2014).
5. Baker (2015).

# Chapter 12

1. Baker (2015).
2. Senge (1990).
3. A wicked problem is a problem that is difficult or impossible to solve because of incomplete, contradictory, and changing requirements that are often difficult to recognize.

# Chapter 13

1. Baker (2014).
2. Baker (2015).

# Chapter 14

1. Baker (2015).
2. http://blog.readytomanage.com/top-10-most-valued-job-skills/

# Chapter 15

1. https://engageforsuccess.org/culture-and-working-environment/job-crafting/
2. Petrou, Demerouti, Peeters, Schaufeli, and Hetland (2012).
3. Berg, Dutton, and Wrzesniewski (2007).
4. Wrzesniewski, Berg, and Dutton (2010).
5. Caldwell and O'Reilly (1990).
6. Halbesleben (2010).
7. Dubbelt, Demerouti, and Rispens (2019).
8. Dutton and Wrzesniewski (2020).

# Chapter 16

1. Wrzesniewski and Dutton (2001).
2. Srivastava and Chamberlain (2005).

# Chapter 17

1. Contact Dr. Tim Baker at tim@winnersatworkcom.au
2. Contact Dr. Tim Baker at tim@winnersatworkcom.au

# References

Baker, T.B. 2009. *The 8 Values of Highly Productive Companies: Creating Wealth from a New Employment Relationship.* Brisbane: Australian Academic Press.

Baker, T.B. 2014. *Attracting and Retaining Talent: Becoming an Employer of Choice.* London: Palgrave Macmillan.

Baker, T.B. 2015. *The End of the Job Description: Shifting from a Job-Focus to a Performance.* London: Palgrave Macmillan.

Baker, T.B. 2015. *The New Influencing Toolkit: Capabilities to Communicate with Influence.* London: Palgrave Macmillan.

Baker, T.B. 2017. *Performance Management for Agile Organizations: Overthrowing the Eight Management Myths that Hold Businesses Back.* London: Palgrave Macmillan.

Baker, T.B. 2021. *Winning Teams: The Eight Characteristics of High Performing Teams.* Brisbane: WINNERS-at-Work.

Baker, T.B., and A.C. Warren. 2015. *Conversations at Work: Promoting a Culture of Conversation in the Changing Workplace.* London: Palgrave Macmillan.

Berg, J.M., J.E. Dutton, and A. Wrzesniewski. 2007. "What is Job Crafting and Why Does it Matter?" Retrieved from https://positiveorgs.bus.umich.edu/wp-content/uploads/What-is-Job-Crafting-and-Why-Does-it-Matter1.pdf

Caldwell, D.F., and C.A. O'Reilly. 1990. "Measuring Person-Job Fit with a Profile-Comparison Process." *Journal of Applied Psychology* 75, pp. 648–657.

Campbell, D.J. 2000. "The Proactive Employee: Managing Workplace Initiative." *Academy of Management Executive* 14, no. 3, pp. 52–66.

Castellano, S. 2014. "What's in a Job?" *Training & Development.*

Contact Dr Tim Baker at tim@winnersatworkcom.au

De Smet, A., C. Hewes, and L. Weiss. 2020. "Busting a Management Myth: Empowering Employees Doesn't Mean Leaving them Alone." www.mckinsey.com/business-functions/organization/our-insights/the-organization-blog/busting-a-management-myth-empowering-employees-doesnt-mean-leaving-them-alone#

Dubbelt, L., E. Demerouti, and S. Rispens. 2019. "The Value of Job Crafting for Work Engagement, Task Performance, and Career Satisfaction: Longitudinal and Quasi-Experimental Evidence." *European Journal of Work and Organizational Psychology* 28, no. 3, pp. 300–314.

Dutton, J.E., and A. Wrzesniewski. 2020. "What Job Crafting Looks Like." *Harvard Business Review.*

Gallo, G. 2011. "70% of Your Employees Hate Their Jobs." www.forbes. com/sites/carminegallo/2011/11/11/your-emotionally-disconnected-employees/?sh=17c7e93c42d5

Gardner, H.K., and I. Matviak. July 8, 2020. "7 Strategies for Promoting Collaboration in a Crisis." *Harvard Business Review*.

Goffee, R., and G. Jones. September-October 2000. "Why Should Anyone be Led by You?" *Harvard Business Review*.

Halbesleben, J.R.B. 2010. "A Meta-Analysis of Work Engagement: Relationships with Burnout, Demands, Resources, and Consequences." In *Work Engagement: A Handbook of Essential Theory and Research*, eds. A.B. Bakker and M.P. Leiter, 102–117. New York, NY: Psychology Press.

Ho, M.H.W., P.N. Ghauri, and J.A. Larimo. 2018. "Institutional Distance and Knowledge Acquisition in International Buyer-Supplier Relationships: The Moderating Role of Trust." *Asia Pacific Journal of Management* 35, no. 2, pp. 427–447.

http://blog.readytomanage.com/top-10-most-valued-job-skills/

http://toolbox.hyperisland.com/team-purpose-culture

https://citrix.com/en-au/news/announcements/apr-2020/remote-work-the-new-normal.html

https://en.wikipedia.org/wiki/GROW_model#cite_note-1

https://en.wiktionary.org/wiki/give_a_man_a_fish_and_you_feed_him_for_a_day;_teach_a_man_to_fish_and_you_feed_him_for_a_lifetime

https://engageforsuccess.org/culture-and-working-environment/job-crafting/

Jacobs, S. 2020. "Building Organizations Fit for Humans." *Developing Leaders Quarterly*, no. 35.

Jones, P.A. February 2016. "10 Paradoxes that Will Boggle Your Mind." *Mental Floss*.

Kouzes, J.M., and B.Z. Posner. 2011. The Five Practices of Exemplary Leadership, 2nd ed. San Francisco: Wiley.

Lee, A., S. Willis, and A.W. Tian. 2017. "Empowering Leadership: A Meta-Analytic Examination of Incremental Contribution, Mediation, and Moderation." *Journal of Organizational Behavior* 39, no. 3, pp. 306–325.

Middlemiss, N. 2015. "Encouraging the Elusive Work-Life Balance – are We All Talk?" www.hcamag.com/hr-news/encouraging-the-elusive-worklife-balance--are-we-all-talk-196257.aspx

Nayer, V. April 2, 2014. "A Shared Purpose Drives Collaboration." *Harvard Business Review*.

Patterson, K., J. Grenny, D. Maxfield, and A. Switzler. 2013. *Crucial Accountability: Tools for Resolving Violated Expectations, Broken Commitments, and Bad Behavior*, 2nd ed. New York, NY: McGraw Hill.

Petrou, P., E. Demerouti, M.C.W. Peeters, W.B. Schaufeli, and J. Hetland. 2012. "Crafting a Job on a Daily Basis: Contextual Correlates and the Link to Work Engagement." *Journal of Organizational Behavior 33*, pp. 1120–1141.

Pink, D.H. 2011. *Drive: The Surprising Truth About What Motivates Us*. New York, NY: Riverhead Books.

Senge, P.M. 1990. "The Art and Practice of the Learning Organization." *The New Paradigm in Business: Emerging Strategies for Leadership and Organizational Change*, pp. 126–138.

Senge, P.M. 1999. *The Dance of Change (A Fifth Discipline Resource)*. New York, NY: Random House.

Srivastava, S., and S. Chamberlain. 2005. "Factors Determining Job Retention and Return to Work for Disabled Employees: A Questionnaire Study of Opinions of Disabled People's Organizations in the UK." *Journal of Rehabilitation Medicine* 37, no. 1, pp. 17–22.

Straw, B.M., L.E. Sandelands, and J.E. Dutton. 1981. "Threat Rigidity Effects in Organizational Behavior: A Multilevel Analysis." *Administrative Science Quarterly* 26, no. 4, pp. 501–524.

Wrzesniewski, A., and J.E. Dutton. 2001. "Crafting a Job: Revisioning Employees as Active Crafters of their Work." *Academy of Management Review* 26, no. 2, pp. 179–201.

Wrzesniewski, A., J.M. Berg, and J.E. Dutton. 2010. "Managing Yourself: Turn the Job you have into the Job you Want." *Harvard Business Review* 88, no. 6, pp. 114–117.

www.brightlaw.com.au/draft-code-of-ethics-for-financial-advisers/

www.brightline.org/learning-from-crisis-mode/

www.ccl.org/articles/leading-effectively-articles/closing-the-gap-between-intent-and-impact/

www.gitadaily.com/sutra-6-words-shape-worlds-watch-your-words/

www.goodreads.com/quotes/118880-no-one-cares-how-much-you-know-until-they-know

www.mindtools.com/pages/article/fostering-initiative-team.htm

# About the Author

**Tim Baker** is a thought leader, international consultant, and successful author. Tim is managing director of WINNERS-at-WORK Pty Ltd, which specializes in leadership development and performance (www. winnersatwork.com.au).

He was recently voted one of *The Most Talented Global Training & Development Leaders* by the World HRD Congress, which is awarded by a distinguished international panel of professionals "who are doing extraordinary work" in the field of HRD. In 2018, Tim was a Finalist in the *Learning Professional of the Year* for the Asia Pacific Institute of Learning Professionals Awards. His consulting firm WINNERS-at-WORK Pty Ltd was listed in the *Top 10 Change Management Consulting Service Companies* in APAC 2020 (HR Tech Outlook).

Tim completed his doctoral degree in 2005 at QUT. He has served on QUT Council for over 12 years.

Tim has conducted over 2,430 seminars, workshops, and keynote addresses to over 45,000 people in 12 countries across 21 industry groups and regularly writes for HR industry press. Tim can be contacted at tim@winnersatwork.com.au.

Tim lives in Brisbane, Australia, with his wife Carol. He has two daughters.

## Connect with Tim online

Contact me at tim@winninersatwork.com.au
LinkedIn: www.linkedin.com/in/winnersatwork/
Facebook: www.facebook.com/winnersatworkptyltd
Twitter: https://twitter.com/winnersatwork/
Instagram: www.instagram.com/winnersatwork/
Pinterest: www.pinterest.com.au/winnersatwork/
YouTube: www.youtube.com/c/TimBakerthoughtleader
SlideShare: www.slideshare.net/DrTimBaker

# Index

## OTHER TITLES IN THE HUMAN RESOURCE MANAGEMENT AND ORGANIZATIONAL BEHAVIOR COLLECTION

Michael Provitera, Barry University, Editor

- *A.I. and Remote Working* by Tony Miller
- *Best Boss!* by Duncan Ferguson, Toni M. Pristo, and John Furcon
- *Managing for Accountability* by Lynne Curry
- *Emotional Connection: The EmC Strategy* by Lola Gershfeld and Ramin Sedehi
- *Fundamentals of Level Three Leadership* by James G.S. Clawson
- *Civility at Work* by Lewena Bayer
- *Lean on Civility* by Christian Masotti and Lewena Bayer
- *The Successful New CEO* by Christian Muntean
- *Agility* by Michael Edmondson
- *Strengths Oriented Leadership* by Matt L. Beadle
- *Leadership in Disruptive Times* by Sattar Bawany
- *The Truth About Collaborating* by Dr. Gail Levitt
- *Level-Up Leadership* by Michael J. Provitera
- *Uses and Risks of Business Chatbots* by Tania Peitzker
- *Three Key Success Factors for Transforming Your Business* by Michael Hagemann

# Concise and Applied Business Books

The Collection listed above is one of 30 business subject collections that Business Expert Press has grown to make BEP a premiere publisher of print and digital books. Our concise and applied books are for…

- Professionals and Practitioners
- Faculty who adopt our books for courses
- Librarians who know that BEP's Digital Libraries are a unique way to offer students ebooks to download, not restricted with any digital rights management
- Executive Training Course Leaders
- Business Seminar Organizers

Business Expert Press books are for anyone who needs to dig deeper on business ideas, goals, and solutions to everyday problems. Whether one print book, one ebook, or buying a digital library of 110 ebooks, we remain the affordable and smart way to be business smart. For more information, please visit www.businessexpertpress.com, or contact sales@businessexpertpress.com.

www.ingramcontent.com/pod-product-compliance
Lightning Source LLC
Chambersburg PA
CBHW061201220326
41599CB00025B/4566